'And the leaves of the tree were for the healing of the nations'

# CROXLEY GREEN
# IN THE FIRST WORLD WAR

*The story of a Hertfordshire Village 1914 to 1919*

## Brian Thomson

Cover photos: Edgar Toms courtesy Liz Frow. Croxley Green VAD
Hospital and VAD nurse courtesy Three Rivers Museum Trust.

1

Published in Great Britain by

# Rickmansworth Historical Society

http://rickmansworthhistoricalsociety.btck.co.uk/

First published – 2014


ISBN number 978-0-9544583-3-1




**Printed in the United Kingdom
by Stephen Austin and Sons Ltd.,
Hertford**

# CROXLEY GREEN IN THE FIRST WORLD WAR
## The story of a Hertfordshire Village 1914 to 1919
### Brian Thomson

## CONTENTS

# CONTENTS Page

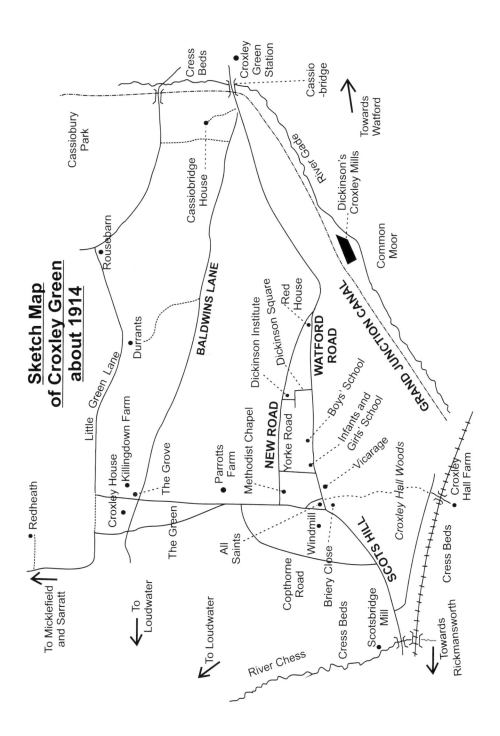

# Sketch Map
## of Croxley Green
## about 1914

Redheath

To Micklefield and Sarratt

To Loudwater

To Loudwater

River Chess

Cress Beds

Scotsbridge Mill

Towards Rickmansworth

Cress Beds

Croxley Hall Farm

SCOTS HILL

Croxley Hall Woods

Briery Close

Windmill

Copthorne Road

All Saints

The Green

Croxley House

Killingdown Farm

The Grove

Parrotts Farm

Methodist Chapel

NEW ROAD

Yorke Road

Vicarage

Infants and Girls' School

Boys' School

WATFORD ROAD

Dickinson Square

Red House

Dickinson Institute

Little Green Lane

Durrants

BALDWINS LANE

Rousebarn

Cassiobridge House

Cassiobury Park

Cress Beds

Croxley Green Station

Cassio-bridge

Towards Watford

River Gade

Dickinson's Croxley Mills

Common Moor

GRAND JUNCTION CANAL

# INTRODUCTION

Croxley Green, south west Hertfordshire, 11 November 1918. If you had been working in Dickinson's paper mill on that Monday morning, you would have been surprised to hear church bells ringing. Along with your workmates, you would have crossed the canal and climbed the lane to the village to find out what was going on. As you walked between the workers' terraces in New Road you would have joined a growing stream of people making their way towards the Green. Outside the Dickinson Institute hospital, convalescing servicemen were delighted that the fighting had stopped and they no longer faced a return to war. School children were processing down the road waving patriotic flags. They stopped outside the hospital and several of the servicemen made short speeches. So did Mr Kennedy, one of the local magistrates, whose wife was the hospital commandant. Everyone cheered.

Then, after the celebrating, if you were of a reflective frame of mind you might pause and look around the village street. There was Mrs Sarah Goodman at number 254 New Road. Before the war, her two young sons enjoyed being part of the Church Lads' Brigade. Both William and John had died in the fighting of 1916. Then there was Alice Randall at number 261, Fred's widow, left on her own to bring up young Freddy, Ada and Edward. You would have known George Mead at number 179 from working at the mill. He had lost two sons, Edwin and Ernest. So had the Newberrys, the publicans at the Duke of York on Watford Road. Neither Samuel nor John would come back from the war. And it wasn't just the ordinary village folk who suffered. The Newall family in the big house at Redheath had lost Leslie and Nigel, both second lieutenants in the army. Sometimes it was the uncertainty that affected people most. There was Mrs Lizzie Toms from Yorke Road still waiting to hear what had become of Edgar, reported missing last March. So many of the village's young men would not come back. By now it must be at least fifty.

This war had affected everyone. Even the vicar, Rev Edward Wells, had joined up as a chaplain. Miss Barker in the big house opposite the church had organised the women to make garments for the Belgian refugees and the troops. Local businesses had been struggling to keep going because almost all the men of military age had been called up. Croxley Mills was employing many more women than before the war.

Perhaps, if the fighting really was over, it would be possible for life to get back to normal. Perhaps you could soon stop worrying if there was enough bread and potatoes to eat. But what was normal after the last four years? There was an election due soon and, for the first time, most women would be able to vote. Was that normal?

********

The aim of this book is to understand the way the war affected the lives of the people of Croxley Green. It takes the form of a chronicle of local events, placed in the context of what was happening nationally and internationally. It begins with a brief survey of the village as it was in 1914, then follows the course of events until the peace agreement of 1919 and concludes by describing how the community commemorated the war. 57 local men are remembered on the war memorial on the Green. Their deaths are marked at the relevant point of the narrative. Special attention is given to the story of the Croxley Green Church Lads who joined up in the early days of the war and were such a source of local pride.

## Acknowledgements and sources

The main sources used are the *West Herts and Watford Observer* (hereafter referred to as the *Observer* or *WO*) and *All Saints' Parish Magazine*, which is only available for part of 1915 and 1916. I have also made use of the records of Croxley Girls' National School for the period. Inevitably, these sources give a partial view of local events and it is hoped that more material will become available as the centenary progresses. Croxley Green was a small part of the *Observer's* area of concern, which in those days stretched from Bushey to Tring. The paper's editorial slant was very much in favour of the war, so there was a lot of attention to those who enlisted and the exploits of the local regiments, the Hertfordshires and Bedfordshires. Reporting from Croxley Green tended to be limited to events associated with the Dickinson Institute and All Saints' Parish Church. No doubt, there was a lot more to the village than is recorded in those sources. Nonetheless, the *Observer* and the church magazine do provide us with important insights into those very different times, when the Great War threw the ordinary people of Croxley Green into the cauldron of international affairs.

I am grateful to Jim Hughes, Richard Lee and Karen Pryse for help in researching the Croxley Green men who died in the war. My thanks are also due to Neil Wheeler who covered some of the same ground in his 1995 report for the Open University, *The First World War Memorials and Soldiers of Croxley Green,* which is lodged in the local studies section of Croxley Green Library.

Family stories help to bring the narrative to life and so I am particularly grateful to Liz Frow for permission to quote from the Toms family correspondence and to Marian Lamsley-Jones and Judy Priest for information about their Croxley Green ancestors. All three have kindly allowed me to make use of photographs from their collections.[1] Three Rivers Museum has conserved some important papers from the Barton-Smith family, including records relating to the VAD hospital at the Dickinson Institute. I am grateful to the Trustees for access to them and permission to use the photographs.

All Saints' church is another important source of local records and I gratefully acknowledge the support of Diane Galloway and the church's permission to use photographs from their collection. I am indebted to Hertfordshire Library Service at Croxley Green, Watford and Hertford for their help in accessing the important material in their collection.

Trevor Spinage has collaborated with me in researching the Croxley Green Church Lads and the 16th King's Royal Rifle Corps and I am grateful for his permission to

1. See Brian Thomson, 'Missing in Action', in *Herts Past and Present,* Issue 23 Spring 2014, pp17-24

make use of his work on their military records.[2] Robin Bolton and George Horner of the Church Lads' and Church Girls' Brigade Historical Group have also been an important source of information.

Heather Falvey has been an invaluable source of advice in preparing this book and I also acknowledge the kind assistance of Greg Hill of Atlantic Publishing.

The cover design, maps and line drawings have been prepared by Alison Lee.

I have endeavoured to trace copyright holders where possible and acknowledge permission from the following to reproduce their photographs (page numbers in brackets):

Hertfordshire Library Service - (9, 32, 33, 37, 52, 136, 145, 147)

Three Rivers Museum Trust - (front and back cover, 10, 11, 13, 22, 23, 28, 29, 39, 41, 43, 88, 89, 90, 93, 99, 102-107, 125, 128, 129, 130, 131)

All Saints' church - (12, 51, 92)

Judy Priest - (20, 72, 74, 75)

Liz Frow - (front cover, 26, 31, 47, 68, 84, 110-114, 118, 119, 135, 143, 149)

Associated Newspapers/Atlantic Publishing - (36, 54, 73, 78, 87, 96, 120)

Atlantic Publishing - (146)

Marian Lamsley-Jones - (135)

National Railway Museum / Science & Society Picture Library - (132)

Patrick Moore - (94)

Brian Thomson - (1, 11, 34, 57, 58, 59, 62, 65, 66, 142)

2. See Trevor Spinage, 'For God, Right and Liberty', in *Watford Observer* 30 June 2006 under the title 'The Brave Heroes of the Somme'

# 1914

## The Village in 1914

In 1914 Croxley Green's population was about 2,400, located midway between the market towns of Watford and Rickmansworth. The settlement comprised a few houses and farms near the Green, a cluster of cottages and shops at the top of Scots Hill and the houses and shops along New Road, which linked the ancient Green with John Dickinson and Co's paper mill by the canal.[3] Croxley Mills were, by far, the largest employer in the village but the countryside was still close by. The local historian, Frank Paddick, described Croxley at around this time as an industrial island surrounded by the great estates of Lords Essex, Clarendon and Ebury (the Cassiobury, Grove and Moor Park estates).[4] The mill and the settlement's small size gave the place a different character from the larger towns of Rickmansworth and Watford and from more agricultural places nearby such as Sarratt and Chorleywood. People knew each other well at work and in their social hours.

*The Dickinson Institute 1915*

The Dickinson Institute on New Road was the hub of community life.[5] It provided facilities for adult education and a wide range of social activities. The buildings were

3. The mill at Croxley was one of several owned by John Dickinson and Co in the Gade valley. In official correspondence the company referred to it as Croxley Mills but local people called it 'the mill'. Both terms are used in this narrative.
4. Frank Paddick, *A Village Boyhood in Croxley Green*, 2012 Rickmansworth Historical Society.
5. This and the following three paragraphs are based on Kelly's Directory 1913/14 and Peacock's Directory 1914

*Paper making machines at Croxley Mills about 1900*

enlarged in 1904 and, in 1914, they comprised a men's club, women's and girls' club, with bath rooms, lads' brigade and club, technical school, laboratory, library, billiard room, recreation and refreshment rooms and an entertainment hall to seat 600 persons. The *Observer* provides some indication of the events staged there. In the first three months of 1914 these included the annual ball organised by the engineers of Croxley Mills, an evening entertainment for Barnardo's Homes, political meetings, the annual dinner of the men's club, a fancy dress ball, an event organised by Croxley Co-operative Society, a whist drive and a concert and dance for the Croxley United Patriots' Benefit Society. No doubt there was plenty more going on that was not recorded in the columns of the press.

The village had three churches, seven pubs (if you include the Half Way House at Cassiobridge) and 'refreshment rooms' in Scots Hill. It boasted two banks, a building society, two insurance agents and a full complement of shops including the Co-operative, a couple of Post Offices, several grocers, butchers, and greengrocers, a newsagents, druggist and drapers. You could buy freshly made bread from two bakers and there were three dairymen to provide milk. If you needed shoes mending there were several bootmakers and a couple of laundries too. There were two hairdressers, a builder and a music teacher. Dr. Evans looked after villagers' health and Constable Haggar kept any unruly elements in check. Most Croxley children attended the elementary schools in Yorke Road and Watford Road. Bearing in mind the number of itinerant tradesmen visiting Croxley Green in those days, it would have been possible to live a pleasant and busy life without leaving the village.

The countryside was close by in the surrounding farms: Parrots, Killingdown, Croxley Hall, Rose Barn, Redheath, Loudwater and Micklefield. In spring the orchards surrounding the Green were a picture. At Easter 1914 the *Observer* commented that the village Green in springtime, famous for its cherry blossom in bordering orchards, looked extremely pretty with its wealth of white blossom (*WO* 18 April 1914). Serving the farming community were a blacksmith and wheelwright. Croxley Green even had its own 'cycle and motor maker' (Mr Kemp of Scots Hill).

Down the hill towards Watford, there were a cluster of businesses alongside the canal and River Gade: a timber merchant, a builder's yard and the watercress farm of the Sansom family. At Scotsbridge mill, towards Rickmansworth, Rexam Ltd made photographic paper and there were more watercress beds in the Chess valley.

*Croxley Hall Farm*

If, however, one had to venture further afield, the London and North Western Railway had opened their branch line from Watford to Croxley Green, near Cassiobridge, in 1912 and there was a regular bus service connecting the village to Watford and Rickmansworth.

The convenience of the railway and the pleasant aspect of the Chess valley meant that Croxley was home to some wealthy commuters even in 1914. For example, Samuel Ingleby Oddie, who lived at Chess Side in Copthorne Road, was a London coroner and William Catesby, of Highfield on Scots Hill, ran a London furniture emporium. They both played an important role in local affairs.

There are a few local residents whose names crop up again and again. Charles Barton-Smith, General Manager of Croxley Mills from 1899 to 1918, was head and shoulders above the others.[6] He was immensely influential in the life of the village as employer, as chairman and treasurer of the Dickinson Institute, as churchwarden at All Saints' and as a member of Rickmansworth Urban District Council. William Richard Woolrych of Croxley House was the main resident landowner. He rather fitted the image of local squire as Justice of the Peace on the Watford Bench, one of the Guardians of the Watford Union Workhouse, chairman of the local Conservative and Unionist Association and chairman of the Rifle Club. Rev Edward Wells was the vicar and, thanks to good links between the church and the newspaper, he appears frequently in their columns. For many local residents the Heads of the Elementary Schools played a formative role. Aricie Clarke was the Head of the Girls' School and

*Charles Barton-Smith*

6. Joan Evans; *The Endless Web: J. Dickinson and Co. 1804 to 1954,* London 1955.

11

H T 'Neggy' Wilson of the Boys'. Neggy was also, for a time, choirmaster at All Saints' church and something of a local institution.[7] Miss Clarke retired in July 1915 and was succeeded by Mildred Stanford.

Life in Croxley was not all work and school. There were football and cricket clubs based at the Dickinson Institute. The Rifle Club had an indoor range at the Institute and an outdoor one near Croxley Mills. The Duke of York pub hosted the Croxley Hotspur quoit club and, if amateur theatricals were more in your line, then there was a Dramatic Club at the Institute too.

*Members of the Church Lads' Brigade at the opening of All Saints' extension in 1908 with the Bishop of Colchester and the Vicar at the time, Rev Donnell*

In view of subsequent events, the Church Lads' Brigade is worth special mention. Nationally, the Anglican church had set up the Brigade in 1891 as a response to the success of the Boys' Brigade.[8] The ethos was quasi-military and the organisation provided exciting opportunities at a time when alternatives were limited. The Croxley Green company was founded on 13 December 1900 as part of the St Albans Battalion and held its meetings at the Dickinson Institute.[9] Charles Barton-Smith was instrumental in setting up the company and in March 1901 he became their Lieutenant (second in command). The Brigade catered for boys and young men between the ages of 13 and 25. In those days most young people left school at 14, so the majority of the Croxley contingent would have been working and many were employed at Croxley Mills. In 1911 the military nature of the Lads was enhanced when the Brigade became a Territorial Cadet Force, which meant it was subject to regulation by the War Office. Although we don't know exactly what happened in Croxley, typical activities included inspection, drill, shooting, first aid, physical exercise, signalling (using morse or semaphore), and bandwork. As a Christian movement Lads were expected to attend Church Parade. Mock battles were often arranged between companies lasting a whole weekend.[10]

7. See Paddick, *Village Boyhood* pp 44-47
8. Robin Bolton. *Looking back, the story of the Church Lads' and Church Girls' Brigade.* Rotherham, Church Lads' and Church Girls' Brigade Historical Group 2002. Accessed from http://www.clcgb.org.uk/historical-group.html
9. Brigade List of Church Lads' Brigade, June 1901.
10. Personal communication from Robin Bolton, Chairman, CLCGB Historical Group, 26 July 2012.

## Local Events in early 1914

The columns of the local press give few clues to the rising international tension in Europe. The political parties held rallies in Croxley Green in January. The local MP, Arnold Ward (Conservative and Unionist), was more concerned with the Irish problem. He urged financial support for the Navy and assistance to Ulster in the form of men to join the Ulster Volunteers against the Liberal Government if necessary. Charles Barton-Smith, who proposed the vote of thanks, struck a note of compromise by hoping that some way out might be found. On the following evening, Ward's Liberal opponent, Mr Le Bas, promoted Lloyd George's programme of pensions, health insurance and social reforms. He attacked Tory policies for tariffs as taxes on food, and pointed out the growing prosperity of Dickinson's mills under the Liberal Government. Le Bas, in line with his party's policies, opposed Ward's proposal of military conscription, accusing him of believing that the only service you could render the country was to blow some Germans' brains out (*WO* 24 January 1914).

As spring moved into summer Croxley enjoyed its normal social round. A concert at the Institute by the Choral Class and Church Choir attracted plaudits for the advance in choral singing achieved by head teachers Miss Clarke and Mr Wilson. Miss May Barton-Smith was busily engaged in arranging a display of drill by the Girls' Gymnasium and an entertainment at the Institute by the Rickmansworth and Croxley Green Girl Guides. On Whit Monday a large number of holiday-makers from London and other parts visited the village and engaged in the fun of the fair.

*May Barton-Smith in Girl Guide uniform*

Both Croxley and Durrants cricket clubs enjoyed a busy programme of fixtures and the Dickinson's Fire brigade (Croxley and Apsley) won the South Midland District competition at Letchworth for the third time. All Saints' church organised an event addressed by a missionary from China. The Band of Hope held their annual tea in the Furze Meadow by Croxley Mills and the Methodists went to Boxmoor for their Sunday School treat.

The *Observer* of 20 June 1914 reported that the Church Lads' Brigade had marched off to camp at Latimer where they enjoyed glorious weather. They stepped out about 50 strong from the Dickinson Institute behind their bugle band, accompanied by their chaplain (Rev E Wells), Captain S Jearrad, Lieutenants S and A Warn and Sergeant-Instructor Denton. The camp followed a strict daily routine punctuated by regular meals. Reveille was at 5.30 am; parade 7 am; tent inspection 9 am; and lights out at 10.30 pm. During their stay, some old members of the Brigade staged a night attack and successfully overran the camp. The Lads attended a Church parade at Chenies and then entertained visitors in the afternoon, including Mr Barton-Smith.

Dickinson's held their 19th Industrial Exhibition at the Institute towards the end of July and, for the first time, they staged athletic sports at the Recreation Ground on the same day. The Company Chairman, Lewis Evans, and his wife presided and gave out the prizes. The exhibition included competitions in woodwork, needlework, cakes, pastries, jams, English composition and recitations, flower arranging and singing. A costume parade preceded the races and the recreation ground was equipped with refreshment stalls, swing-boats and coconut shies. The tug-of-war, in which the Tradesmen bested the Church team after three strenuous pulls, caused special excitement.

## The Outbreak of War

Meanwhile, international events were getting out of hand. Austria, with German support, declared war on Serbia on 28 July. Russia mobilised its army in support of Serbia, thus entangling her French ally. On 4 August, Germany invaded Belgium and Britain declared war on Germany.

War did not come as a surprise because tension with Germany had been a concern for years. However, it is one thing to acknowledge the possibility of war and quite another to confront the real thing. The general mood of the country was in favour of war and the announcement was met by cheering crowds in London. However, not everyone locally was in favour. The *Observer* records that, on Monday 4 August, the Watford and District Free Church Council called an extraordinary meeting at which they approved a resolution calling on the Prime Minister and Foreign Secretary to preserve the nation in a position of strict neutrality (*WO* 8 August 1914).

The *Observer* made an extensive review of the local response to the declaration of war and commented on the lack of nationalistic displays and 'mafficking'.[11]  In contrast, the paper felt that people were gravely determined to do all that could be done to assist the Government and to mitigate the necessarily terrible consequences of the struggle.

There is no specific reference in the *Observer* to the mood in Croxley Green. Frank Paddick remembers the patriotic songs played on the gramophone and the conflicting emotions aroused by world events - his mother's fears on the one hand and a New Road neighbour's jingoistic enthusiasm.[12]  No doubt many in Croxley were proud supporters of the British Empire. For example, in All Saints' archive, there is a programme for a 'Grand Patriotic Entertainment' on Empire Day, 24 May 1913, in the hall of the Dickinson Institute. The programme included patriotic music, songs by Kipling accompanied by the Institute band, national dancing by the Gymnasium girls,

11. Uproarious celebrations - originally a reference to rejoicing at the relief of Mafeking. *Oxford English Dictionary*
12. Paddick, Village Boyhood pp. 19-21

a dramatic sketch by the Church Lads' Brigade, not to mention a cantata, 'John Bull and his Trades' by the Institute Dramatic Company.

Each year Empire Day was celebrated by the local schools with ceremonial and a holiday. In May 1914 the head mistress of the Girls' School recorded, 'The girls marched up to the Boys' School at 9 o'clock. Mr Barton-Smith made an appropriate little speech – the children saluted the flag – sang the National Anthem and then returned to School. Special lessons were given on our Empire and in the afternoon a holiday was given'. The tradition continued during the war. In 1917 the head mistress wrote in the log book, 'The girls went to the boys' school to salute the flag and a short Empire address was given by Mr Barton-Smith. At 11 o'clock there was much excitement in the classroom while Britannia, Neptune, sailors, miners, soldiers, munition workers, fishermen etc robed; to say nothing of the dusky hues imparted by burnt cork for India and Africa. Two short plays, "The Last Rally" and "Freedom's Empire" were then given by the upper girls to the rest of the boys and girls in The Boys' playground'.[13]

The Territorials of the Hertfordshire Regiment and Hertfordshire Yeomanry reported for duty. Amongst the reservists called up were H Matthews (Scottish Rifles) and L Keen (Royal Scottish Fusiliers) from Croxley Green Post Office. The military commandeered lorries, including four from Benskins the brewers in Watford, and horses. The Watford Voluntary Aid Detachment (the ambulance corps which served with the Territorials) was reported to be ready for service. Hertfordshire Boy Scouts volunteered to help deliver dispatches or guard bridges.[14] Travellers were warned that the movement of troops could disrupt the trains.

But not everyone in West Hertfordshire responded positively. People rushed to stock their larders, resulting in rising prices and scarcity. The people of Hitchin were so incensed that they attacked the home of one of the town's grocers. Nothing so riotous occurred in our corner of the county. But a Watford fishmonger, Allen Anker, took out a front page advertisement to reassure the public that every effort would be made to serve them as cheaply as possible. He explained that, while the deep sea fishing fleet was kept in harbour for fear of the German navy, some fish would be scarce, but herrings would be plentiful because Britain could no longer export them to Europe, and so they would be available for the local consumer. The *Observer* condemned the selfish and cowardly people in the district who had raided the grocers' shops and caused prices to soar. Local journalists surveyed the supply situation for meat, flour, bread, milk, coal, petrol, water, electricity and gas. They found that normal supplies could be maintained for most commodities and there was no justification for panic.

Of course, in the excitement everyone wanted to know what was going on. Newspaper sales were at record levels and it was announced that official telegrams about the war would be displayed at chief Post Offices.

13. Croxley Green National School Log Books 1914 and 1917
14. Frank Brittain, *The Role of Hertfordshire Scouts on the Home Front during WWI*, 1 January 2014, Hertfordshire Scouts.

## Call to Arms

The *Observer* of 15 August published the first recruiting advertisement for volunteers:

**CALL TO ARMS**
**Men between 19 & 30 years of age desirous of joining**
**LORD KITCHENER'S**
**NEW ARMY**
**Should apply at once at Clarendon Hall**

The MP for West Herts, Arnold Ward, set an example by leaving Watford for the war as a Lieutenant in the local reserve cavalry regiment, the Hertfordshire Yeomanry.

Then, as the British Expeditionary Force was facing defeat by the Germans at Mons, 50 Special Constables were sworn in at Croxley Green by Mr Woolrych and his fellow JPs. Meanwhile, Charles Barton-Smith announced that the Croxley rifle ranges, the open-air one at Croxley Mills and also the one in the Institute, would be thrown open for all men over 18 who wanted to learn to shoot. Rifles and ammunition were provided free of charge. According to the *Observer*, large numbers from the Mills availed themselves of the opportunity with instruction from members of the Rifle Club. Meanwhile, in Croxley village, as in many other places, women were meeting in private houses to make garments for soldiers and sailors.

## Croxley Mills

The management of Dickinson's Ltd. was determined to avoid disruption to the business. Charles Barton-Smith circulated to staff on 26 August a leaflet entitled 'Croxley Mills: War Conditions' which was marked private and personal.[15] It shows a good deal of foresight about the local impact of the war. The leaflet reveals a company that was not only concerned about business but also with its national contribution and, in a paternalistic fashion, with the welfare of the village and the private lives of its employees. The text is worth quoting in full:

> The condition of the Mill as regards Materials and Chemicals is fairly satisfactory and every effort will be made to keep running and at full time. All depends on the length of the War and our ability to obtain further supplies when our present stock of materials is exhausted. The price of everything we now buy is increased and the greatest economy needs to be exercised in every department of the Mill. Orders will fall off in some directions but if our Export trade can be carried on we are fairly confident of sufficient business for some time.

> A number of our men have joined the Colours; provision will be made for the wives of those married and also for any dependent on those called out. In all cases their posts in the Mill will be kept open for them and on their return they will each be presented with a month's wages. The Mill will be working with a

15. From the collection of Three Rivers Museum Trust

reduced staff but I am confident that every one will do their best by extra effort and energy to keep up the efficiency of the Mill.

The Mill rifle range has been placed at the disposal of the men of the Village and Mill for instruction in Rifle shooting, ammunition being supplied free to men of all ages who will fit themselves by Rifle shooting and drill for the service of their country. A body of 50 Special Constables has been sworn in at Croxley Green to relieve the Police and protect property if needed.

The War, if extended over a long period, will certainly result in much want and distress in the neighbourhood and possibly among ourselves, and every one should prepare for the possibilities of the future by exercising the greatest economy in their private expenditure but at the same time helping others by promptly paying our debts and meeting our just obligations. The greatest attention should be paid to allotment gardening. Free garden allotments can now be had on the Furze Field.

Local branches of the Prince of Wales' Fund have been started to relieve distress when the need arises. A Mill collection will be arranged shortly, and it is hoped that everyone will subscribe according to their means.

The Institute buildings have been offered to the Red Cross Society for Hospital purposes, and if accepted, the inhabitants of Croxley Green will be asked to provide the necessary furnishing and labour to carry it on. In association with the Red Cross Society, garments for our Soldiers and Sailors are being made by the women of the Village.

In the anxious times which are before us we shall all have to make sacrifices, keep calm under disaster, assist each other in any way we can, and do everything in our power for our Soldiers and Sailors and those dependent on them.

Charles Barton-Smith, Manager

On 5 September the *Observer* reported what they described as John Dickinson and Co's patriotic offer in response to the national emergency. The Chairman, Lewis Evans, had issued the following notice:

> Messrs John Dickinson & Co Ltd, feel that it is their chief duty to endeavour to keep their works going; subject to this, they desire to urge the men in their employment to enlist in His Majesty's Forces. But, as it is not in the best interests of our country that any should leave whose absence will stop the work of others, all who desire to enlist should first consult the foreman of the department. Places will be kept open for all those who leave with the consent of the company. Half-wages will be given to all who are married or who have dependents, and one quarter wages to all unmarried men, and a bonus of one month's wages or salary will be given to all who return at the end of the war.[16]

16. Evans, The Endless Web p.178 and WO 5 September 1914

Such was the general enthusiasm for war that the response was immediate and between 90 and 100 Dickinson men asked for permission to enlist, in addition to the Reservists and Territorials previously called up. By the end of the war 1,604 Dickinson employees had enlisted, from all their plants, and 225 (about one in seven) lost their lives in the conflict.[17]

There were wild rumours that essential imports for the mill would be stopped, so steps were taken to collect and store waste materials that might be put to use. Croxley Mills were fortunate not to have any of their motor vans commandeered but the management lent them to the Hertfordshire Territorial Force Association for various military uses.

Once the initial panic was over, the mill settled down to wartime production. New lines were introduced such as photographic paper and other papers which were likely to be scarce, for example because of restrictions on imports. The mill staff even made small quantities of munitions including trench mortar bombs and shells. The management tried to substitute new materials so as to conserve the stock of imported wood pulp and esparto grass. They took on a large staff of women workers to sort waste paper, which was collected by motor vans from a wide area.

---

# FIGHTING ON THE WESTERN FRONT IN 1914

The German invasion of Belgium on 4 August took the Allies by surprise and the small British Expeditionary Force had no choice but to retreat in the face of overwhelming force at Mons on 20 August. It was not until 4 September that the Allies were able to halt the German advance, just short of Paris, at the first battle of the Marne. The Allied counterattack forced the Germans back. Each side tried to outflank the other to the west in what became known as the race to the sea. By November, when the Germans tried unsuccessfully to dislodge the British positions at Ypres, the defences of both armies had coalesced in trench lines from Dunkirk to Switzerland. The remains of the Belgian army held positions near the coast, the British took over southwards to Arras and the French armies held the remainder.

---

## The Enlistment Campaign

At times the atmosphere verged on the hysterical. Spy stories were rife and anyone or anything connected to Germany was the subject of suspicion and abuse. The press, politicians and church pulpits were all full of exhortations to enlist and condemnation of those slow to do so. The *Observer* was no exception yet it did

---

17. See for this and next two paragraphs, John Dickinson & Co. Ltd, *Croxley Mills, War Time in a Paper Mill 1914-18*, mimeo in local collection of Croxley Green Library. The preface ends with the initials CBS so Charles Barton-Smith was probably responsible for compiling this material.

publish a letter from T Moffet of Oxhey which struck a more moderate note *(WO* 12 September 1914). He implored the local clergy to refrain from using their pulpits for war sermons. In particular, he urged preachers not to hold up to scorn, ridicule and insults every young man who was not in uniform. Moffet pointed out that thousands of men were unable to enlist on account of their duties or physical disabilities. He felt that the white feather crusade and suggestions of cowardice in street and pulpit was senseless and the cause of endless trouble, misery and worry to men with good reasons for not joining up.

On 17 September, the Earl of Essex presided at the first open air meeting of the recruitment campaign in Watford. During a bellicose speech he reminded his audience that local man, General Smith-Dorrien, had saved the Army.[18] He hoped Hertfordshire would breed more like him (*WO* 19 September 1914). There was loud applause. After the speeches a group of young men lined up ready to receive the rosette badge from the Earl. The majority of them were from Croxley Green. In all 36 names were taken.

During September and the following months, while the armies were digging in on the Western Front, many of the *Observer's* column-inches were given over to the 'Local Patriotic Roll' of those who had joined up. The roll included many names from Croxley Green. The records at All Saints' church list 109 local men who joined the forces during 1914.[19]

## Church Lads' Brigade

At about the same time, the Commandant of the Church Lads' Brigade, Field Marshall Lord Grenfell, called for the Brigade to form a battalion from members past and present.[20] Grenfell was an old colonial soldier who had been a colleague of Kitchener's during the war in Sudan. This battalion became the 16th King's Royal Rifle Corps (16th KRRC), whose formation was lauded by Rev Edgar Rogers with nationalistic and religious hyperbole. He claimed that the war had called out all that is best in the Christian manhood of the Empire against the 'paganism' of Germany and the Church Lads' Brigade had achieved a feat without parallel since the days of Crecy and Agincourt, the formation of a complete battalion of churchmen.[21] Fortunately, the recruits themselves, although enthusiastic, were more level-headed and practical in their outlook.

There were well over 40 Church Lads of military age in Croxley Green and most of them worked at Croxley Mills.[22] Charles Barton-Smith was all in favour of them

18. Sir Horace Lockwood Smith-Dorrien (1858-1930), born in Berkhamsted, was in charge of the 2nd Corps of the British Expeditionary Force and managed to stop the German pursuit after the defeat of Mons at Le Cateau. Stephen Badsey, *Oxford Dictionary of National Biography*, OUP 2004.
19. See the roll of honour of those from Croxley Green who enlisted, which is installed in All Saints' Parish Church. The monument was created in 1917 and is known as the All Saints' war shrine.
20. See *Oxford Dictionary of National Biography*: Grenfell, Francis Wallace, first Baron Grenfell (1841–1925), army officer, by H de Watteville, rev James Falkner.
21. E Rogers.*The Church Lads' Battalion of the King's Royal Rifle Corps: a Unique Achievement of the Church*. From 'The Sign', Mowbray (1915).
22. See Lynn Macdonald, *Somme*, Michael Joseph, 1983, pp.142-143

*Croxley Green Church Lads' Brigade in the early 1900s. Charles Barton-Smith is at the centre of the back row.*

enlisting without delay and they rushed to do so. One of them was his son, Arthur. The 'Local Patriotic Roll' in the *Observer* of 26 September 1914 recorded their names with approval. One of the group, Jack Beament, recalled that they all passed their medicals, even Charlie Rogers who was almost blind in one eye. Their calling-up papers arrived soon afterwards and the mill laid on a lorry to take them from the Red House pub up to Kingsway in London, where they enlisted. Then the Lads marched to Paddington station, stepping out like soldiers while Jack Brown played 'The Girl I Left Behind Me' on his flute. Boarding the train, and prepared to go anywhere in the country, they were surprised to find that their destination was Denham, just seven miles from Croxley Green. Their training camp was on the estate of Major C E Wyld, later Colonel and Commanding Officer of the Church Lads' Brigade battalion, 16th KRRC.

The *Observer's* 26 September edition reported Croxley's first casualty of the war. Private W Eames, 4th Dragoon Guards, and an employee of Croxley Mills, was wounded at Mons. The paper was proud to announce that he was about to return to his regiment, determined to go again to the front.

Charles Barton-Smith presided at the annual business meeting of the Dickinson Institute on 23 September. The Institute and its Sick Benefit Club agreed to keep enlisted soldiers and sailors as members during the war and to pay their subscriptions for them. The Sick Benefit Club also agreed that servicemen could share equally with other members at the Christmas distribution.

The plight of Belgian refugees excited particular sympathy because of the horrors they had suffered during the German advance. The parishioners of All Saints' celebrated their harvest thanksgiving with gifts of food for the refugees. According to the *Observer*, which also commented on the high standard of singing by the choir trained by 'Neggy' Wilson, there was a splendid response. The old chancel became well stocked with provisions which the vicar announced would be sent over the following week. In November a group of Belgians attended an event at the Dickinson Institute and they were given a warm welcome.

It wasn't just raw recruits for the army that were needed. On 30 October, Edward Warn and George Kerr, both members of the Croxley Mills Fire Brigade and Ambulance, left for service in France with the British Red Cross Society. The company Chairman, Lewis Evans, who was also High Sheriff, and employees gave them an enthusiastic send-off. The Dickinson Institute continued to find ways to support the national effort. Winners of a whist drive in November agreed to send their prizes of cigarettes to soldiers at the front. Charles Barton-Smith presided over a well-attended meeting at the Institute to form a training company of volunteers for men unable to join the army.

---

## CROXLEY GREEN'S FIRST MAN KILLED IN ACTION

**Corporal Arthur Toms** was killed on 3 November 1914. He lies buried at Le Touquet Railway Crossing cemetery, some 10 miles south of Ypres. Arthur served in the 1st Battalion, Rifle Brigade. 27 other members of the 1st Rifle Brigade are buried with him, all victims of fierce German attacks on the 11th Infantry Brigade (4th Division) during the first battle of Ypres. Arthur was 29 when he died and the son of Edward and Sarah Toms of 49 Dickinson Square. He was born in Croxley on 25 September 1885 and baptised in All Saints' church. Arthur's father was a papermaker at Croxley Mills and several of his siblings worked there too.

---

### 16th Battalion, King's Royal Rifle Corps: Church Lads in Training

Arthur Barton-Smith kept a diary of his time training at Denham and it seems that life as a trainee Rifleman had something of the atmosphere of a Church Lads' camp – at least to start with. The surroundings were familiar.[23] They knew the locality and when they got leave they could go home easily along the the six miles or so of canal towpath. Arthur left a bicycle at Mrs Burrell's house where he was billeted to start with. The Lads were welcomed by the local people and used the local library and pubs as their 'club' where they could go and read the papers and unwind. Initially, the Croxley boys were all together in 'A' Company.[24] Two sections (about 30) slept and messed

23. Arthur Barton-Smith's diaries, Three Rivers Museum Trust.
24. Battalions in the British Army were normally composed of four companies of about 220 men.

*16th Battalion KRRC recruits on parade*

together in a barn known as 'Pig Sty View'. The *Observer* reported on 14 November that the Croxley contingent spent some pleasant evenings. There was a concert with Rifleman Warn in the chair, when they entertained Lads from Chesham and planned that, when the battalion entered Germany, the Croxley and Chesham Lads would be the first across the border.

It seems that their activities may have become a bit riotous because Arthur records soon afterwards that the Croxley Lads were split up. He and a couple of others were transferred to 'B' Company and others to 'D' company. His new CO, Captain Thomas said 'You're the Croxley chaps? Well you have been sent to this Company with a very bad reputation. If you work well we shall get on alright but if I hear anything in the way of complaints from you, I shall not forget where you come from.'

Things at Denham started getting a bit more serious. It rained and Arthur recorded on 5 December that they had to cope with liquid mud up to their ankles. They gained lots of digging practice, drilling and route marching. Their first rifles started arriving but not for everyone. On 7 December Arthur lamented, 'We companies who have no rifles have now been served out with scout staves which we have to treat in every way like rifles. If the Germans hear of this, their cartoons will have the time of their life – and depict us as marching with broomsticks'.

Meanwhile, a strict medical examination resulted in three Croxley lads being discharged, Herbert Element (bad throat and feet), Fred (Sol) Quelch (varicose veins) and Alf Warn (bad feet) (Arthur Barton-Smith's diaries and *WO* 9 Jan 1915). Further examination of Herbert's military record shows that it was not his feet that were responsible for his discharge. After only three weeks training he spent the rest of the time in hospital and was not considered fit to be inoculated. The medical board found that he suffered from 'neurasthenia', an ill-defined nervous disorder which was later diagnosed in many soldiers returning from the trenches with 'shell shock'. Herbert was given the silver war badge to acknowledge his disability.

However, life for the recruits was not all grind. They formed a battalion orchestra under the leadership of Croxley's Arthur Raggett. The *Observer* reported that regular musical evenings in the camp concert room were greatly appreciated. Rifleman Raggett, who had been given full charge of the band, had proved himself to be a capable instructor (*WO* 13 March 1915). There was also some relief from the weather when the battalion was able to occupy wooden huts, constructed in December.

The young soldiers were required to attend lectures designed to boost their morale and keep them focussed on defeating the enemy. But it didn't always have the desired effect. On 10 December Arthur Barton-Smith recorded that they went to Uxbridge to listen to 'Sir Somebody Somebody on the British Empire' and why it went to war. He complained in his diary, 'Why will these folk keep drumming into our ears the fact that we are fighting in a just cause? That is why most of us enlisted. Why try and convince the convinced? And now that we are soldiers what does the cause matter? We have pledged ourselves to our country and we will of necessity fight, be her cause never so bad.'

*A group of Arthur Barton-Smith's comrades from the 16th KRRC*

23

# 1915

In the early months of the new year, the *Observer's* pages were full of recruiting cartoons and exhortations for men to join up in Kitchener's New Army. Many different ways were tried to exert moral pressure on men to join up. For example, one cartoon showed an embarrassed family man being interrogated by his seven-year old son some time in the future, 'Daddy why weren't <u>you</u> a soldier during the war?'. Meanwhile, public enthusiasm to support the troops continued at a high level and the newspaper ran a campaign to send cigarettes to the boys in the front line.

People in Croxley Green tried, as far as they could, to maintain the pre-war pattern of life. Croxley Mills held its nineteenth annual New Year's tea for over 300 children of staff. After tea they were entertained with a programme organised by Miss Barton-Smith. It included music by the Institute band, and two plays, 'Cinderella', by the village children, and the 'Slave of the Lamp' by the local Girl Guides (*WO* 9 January 1915).

## Croxley Green War Working Party

People were keen to provide practical support for the war effort. Miss Barker, of Briery Close, had convened a War Working Party. She reported to the *Observer* that meetings were held weekly from the outbreak of war, and they intended to carry them on to the end. The working party was chiefly composed of residents who were unable to provide expensive materials but gladly gave their work and time. Special thanks had been received from Lady Salisbury for the quality of what they had achieved. Hundreds of garments – socks, mittens, underclothing, comforts for the wounded, scarves and mufflers, and clothing of all kinds for the Belgians - had already been sent. They were sending a further collection of garments for British soldiers and sailors, including the sick and wounded, for the distressed Belgians in Holland, and, hopefully, for British prisoners of war in Germany (*WO* 13 February 1915).

Perhaps the war had something to do with the record number of communicants at the Easter services at All Saints' church. But there were attempts to strike a lighter note too. On Easter Monday the usual village fair took place on the green and at Watford Palace Theatre, Marie Lloyd, queen of comediennes, was appearing twice nightly with new songs and Paris gowns.

At the Easter Vestry meeting the church re-elected Charles Barton-Smith as people's warden, a post he had held for almost 20 years. Later in April, the twentieth Industrial Exhibition took place at the Dickinson Institute. It was a lower key affair than usual and the exhibits were entirely local. The aim was to display the results of the winter's technical classes and the children's competitions.

# GALLIPOLI AND THE DARDANELLES

Turkey entered the war on the side of the Central Powers on 1 November 1914. The British Indian Army and the Russians attacked the Ottoman Empire in Mesopotamia and Armenia respectively. British Forces repulsed a Turkish attack on the Suez Canal in early February 1915. The British Government planned a decisive attack to force Turkey out of the war. First a fleet attempted to force a passage through the Dardanelles straits on 18 March but failed to penetrate the minefields. Then British, French, Australian and New Zealand troops landed on the Gallipoli peninsula on 25 April 1915. The Allies failed to break out of the beachhead and the troops were evacuated in December 1915 after suffering heavy losses.

The Dardanelles and Gallipoli campaigns cost the deaths of two Croxley men.

**Signalman John Henry Gardner** died on 18 March 1915. He was a crewman of HMS Inflexible, a battlecruiser, and the flagship of the Dardanelles operation. On 18 March, while part of the fleet attempted to force the Dardanelles Narrows, she was hit twice by gunfire from Turkish forts and nine crew members were killed; later the same day, she struck a mine and was forced to withdraw. John was 24 when he died and the son of John Gardner of 275 New Road. Appropriately, his father was a gardener. The family were living in Watford in 1901 and 1911. By 1911 John Henry was already in the Navy as a signalman on HMS Implacable.

**Able Seaman Robert Francis Duley, RNVR**, died at Gallipoli on 3 May 1915. He fought as an infantryman in the Anson Battalion of the Royal Naval Division. Duley does not have a grave but is remembered on the Helles Memorial to the missing, Gallipoli. Duley is not listed on the Croxley Green war memorial but was remembered at the All Saints' service in November 1915. The *Observer* mentioned him on their 'local patriotic roll' of those enlisting on 3 October 1914. According to the paper he lived at 285 New Road. Robert Duley was born on 18 January 1888 at Warborough, Oxfordshire. In 1911 he was living as a boarder at 43 New Road with the Taylor family. He worked as a domestic gardener. When he was killed, his next of kin was his step-mother, Mary Duley, who lived in Egham, Surrey.

### Croxley Green Girls' School

In April the Girls' School won the shield for the highest attendance in the County. In the year ended January 1915 there were 120 girls on the roll and average attendance was 119. However, things changed soon afterwards. Miss Clarke, the head mistress, noted in the log book on 30 April that an epidemic of measles had broken out in the village. Attendances dropped to 63.7% in May, 'The lowest we have ever had'. The school closed for a whole week at Whitsun instead of Monday and Tuesday as normal, because of measles.[25]

At the end of the summer term Miss Clarke retired from the Girls' School. Her final entry in the log book on 28 July reads, 'I, Aricie Clarke, resigned my post as Head Mistress of this School after nearly forty years' service.' She had been involved with the school since it was started by All Saints' Church in 1875. Since then she had experienced the overcrowding which resulted from the expansion of Croxley Mills in the 1880s, the extension of the buildings and the separation of the older boys into their own school in 1894. The *Observer* quoted the following appreciation from All Saints' Parish magazine, probably written by the vicar who was chair of the school trustees (*WO* 10 July 1915):

> Everyone in the parish will be sorry to hear that Miss Clarke is retiring at the end of this term. The managers would, of course, like to ask her to continue her work, but have refrained from doing so, as Miss Clarke, though still strong and in good health, feels that she would like to have some rest after her many years of hard work and responsibility, and so we feel we must comply with her wishes, and not be selfish in trying to persuade her against her better judgment. It is by no means easy to realise all that Miss Clarke has done in shaping the lives and characters of many hundreds of people in our village. An able teacher, with a wonderful gift of discipline, well able to keep up with the march of educational progress, Miss Clarke has been second to none in efficiency. But still more valuable has been the influence of her example. No one could be more conscientious and upright, no one could be more just in dealing with her pupils. Then there has been her religious instruction, careful, reverent, and carrying conviction, because it was given by one who led a singularly blameless life. It would be difficult to over-estimate the value of work such as this, which has been so quietly and systematically going on all these years. Everyone will be pleased to hear that Miss Clarke intends to live on in Croxley after her retirement.

Mildred Stanford succeeded as head mistress in September. She had previously taught at the Boys' School. In her first entry in the log book she commented, 'the late Head Mistress, Miss Clarke, had left everything in excellent order, so the change has not proved as formidable as I expected'. There were 134 girls on the books, divided between standards four to seven, and Miss Stanford had the assistance of two uncertificated teachers, Misses Vincent and Jones, and one supplementary teacher, Miss Clappen.

Mildred Stanford

25. Croxley Green National School Log Book 1915

# SECOND BATTLE OF YPRES

The beginning of 1915 saw a series of attacks by both sides in Flanders and Picardy. The Germans attacked Ypres at the end of April and forced the British to pull back their defensive line closer to the town.

**Rifleman Fredrick John Walker** died on 10 May. He served in the 4th Battallion of the King's Royal Rifle Corps and was 27 when he died. He has no known grave and is remembered on the Menin Gate at Ypres. The Commonwealth War Graves Commission records Walker as the son of Rosa Alice Hack of Fernley Cottage, Croxley Green. At the 1911 census Arthur and Rosa Hack lived on their own at 225 New Road. According to *All Saints' magazine* of July 1915, John Walker had lived for many years with Mr and Mrs Hack, who regarded him almost as a son. He originally came from Great Missenden and had been in the army for some years.

## Death of Mr Woolrych

William Richard Woolrych of Croxley House, one of the most prominent local figures, died after a short illness on 19 May at the age of 78 years. There was a sense of the passing of an era. The family had lived at Croxley House since 1794 and he was born there on 6 January 1837, the year of the accession of Queen Victoria. After training as a barrister, he worked in the Legacy and Succession Office in Somerset House. He was married on 18 May 1870, to Dorothea Louisa, daughter of Mr Humphrey Harper Burchell-Herne of Bushey Grange. They had no children.

The *Observer's* obituarist regarded Woolrych as an English country gentleman and public servant (*WO* 22 May 1915). The newspaper commented that he and his wife were the leading residents of Croxley Green and showed unfailing courtesy and service to the community. He became a magistrate in 1876 and sat frequently on the Watford Bench. As a Justice of the Peace, he acted as Guardian of the Poor for the Watford Union and as a member of the old Watford Sanitary Authority. In 1894, when the Local Government Act came into force, he was elected Rural District Councillor for Rickmansworth and held that office until he died. He had also represented Rickmansworth on the County Council from 1892. William Woolrych was a staunch Conservative, and for many years was the vice-president of the Watford and West Herts Conservative Association, and Chairman of the Croxley Branch. He was patron of many local clubs and invited the organisers of local meetings to make use of the grounds of Croxley House. The paper concluded that he would be greatly missed.

The members of the Watford bench paid tribute to Mr Woolrych for his forty years service and commented on his kindness and his sympathetic attitude to the poor. Lady Ebury, Chairman of the Board of Guardians, noted that he had been a member of the Board longer than anyone and said that she looked upon him as her ideal of an English country gentleman – beloved of his poorer neighbours, a dear friend, unassuming and quiet.

The well-attended funeral service took place on 25 May at All Saints' church before the cremation at Golders Green, and the subsequent interment of the ashes at Bushey Churchyard. The *Observer* commented on the impressive and memorable funeral cortege (*WO* 29 May 1915).

## 16th Battalion, King's Royal Rifle Corps: Church Lads in training

*Field Marshal Grenfell and the Archbishop inspect the 16th KRRC - still equipped with staves.*

Meanwhile, the Croxley Church Lads continued training with their colleagues in the 16th King's Royal Rifle Corps. They received some ecclesiastical recognition when the Archbishop of Canterbury, Randall Davidson, and Field Marshall Lord Grenfell reviewed the battalion on 22 February. Two days later it snowed but, as Arthur Barton-Smith records, that did not stop the battalion's programme of field exercises. Nonetheless, it took time before they felt real soldiers. It was not until March 1915, just before the Battalion moved to Rayleigh in Essex, that Arthur received his uniform.

His billet in Rayleigh enjoyed the comfort of a spring bed. He met up with some of his Croxley pals for a turn of whist; Jim Lyons, Arthur Hobbs, Jack Brown, Oliver Atkins and Bill Warn. They all seemed well settled except Bill Warn who reflected ruefully that he was staying with two Wesleyan old maids who frowned on alcohol. On 29 March Arthur wrote in his diary that he had spent the day digging trenches. 'The hour's rest we spent under a sunny hedge, well sheltered from the wind, and facing the Thames. It is a fine life, is a soldier's! We shall soon be quite brown.' Then on 1 April he spent the day bayonetting sacks. 'It is more tiring than a day's barrow trundling - who said a soldier's life is all play!'

Nationally, the Church Lads' Brigade took great pride in the numbers enlisting. The periodical 'The Brigade' issued a supplement, 'On Duty', in February 1915 with the

*16th KRRC on parade. Location uncertain - Rayleigh?*

names of all those who had joined up. There are 41 names from Croxley Green of whome 32 were in the 16th KRRC.[26]

## First anniversary of the War

On 7 August, the *Observer* reviewed the vast changes that had come upon West Herts over the year and looked forward to glorious victory. The paper claimed that the district had a proud patriotic record, for example in the numbers of recruits for the armed forces. The county regiments, the Hertfordshires and the Bedfordshires, had excelled in the fighting. Two Hertfordshire men had gained the Victoria Cross. £7,000 had been raised in Watford for war assistance funds. The ladies had made a notable contribution by providing necessities and comforts for the troops. Meanwhile, divisive local issues had faded into insignificance and sporting activities had taken a back seat. The anniversary had seen many local patriotic meetings. In Watford, Lords Clarendon and Essex presented awards to members of the Primrose League and the National Patriotic Association.[27] Meanwhile, in Rickmansworth, the local Friendly Societies paraded to benefit local Red Cross Hospitals for wounded soldiers, including the one at St. Augustine's Hall. The Croxley Branch of the United Patriots' Benefit Society joined in, proudly carrying its banner.[28]

26. See Appendix 1 for the list and what became of them.
27. The Primrose League was formed by admirers of Disraeli in 1883 to promote Conservative Party principles and imperialism. See http://www.britishmuseum.org/explore/highlights/highlight_objects/cm/p/primrose_league_badge.aspx (viewed 9 April 2013)
28. The United Patriots' Benefit Society was one of several Friendly Societies active in Croxley Green. The Society was set up in 1843, supported by the Chartists and Consolidated Trades Union. It was designed to provide poorer members of society with insurance based on their contributions. See I. J. Prothero, *Radical Artisans in England and France*, Cambridge University Press 1997 p. 152.

## More volunteers needed

Amidst talk of how to resist a possible German invasion, Kitchener gave official recognition to a Volunteer Training Corps (VTC) for men who had a genuine reason for not joining the army such as their age, their occupation or lack of fitness.[29]   They were expected to carry out regular drill and learn how to shoot. The *Observer's* Editor commented with pride on the way that local veterans had established a Hertfordshire Volunteer Regiment (*WO* 7 August 1915). They had undertaken arduous training and even provided their own uniforms and equipment, because of the lack of support from the government.   The Croxley Committee appealed for recruits, especially those aged 16 to 19, to bear their part in defence of their homes (*WO* 5 June 1915).   The *Observer* reported that the local VTC went for a route march, headed by the Dickinson Institute band (*WO* 19 June 1915).

By the middle of 1915, many Croxley men had already joined the forces and the July issue of the *All Saints' Parish Magazine* reported that Miss Ricketts and Mr P. Ricketts had carefully compiled a new Roll of Honour of those who had enlisted.  It hung on the church door and included 160 names.

As the year went on there were growing concerns about how to gain more recruits for the Army. The *Observer's* editor felt that there were plenty of young men still at home who should join up (*WO* 2 October 1915). Moreover, those men not of military age should learn drill and the use of arms, so that they could be prepared for any emergency at home.

In this context, the Croxley Rifle Club took on a special significance and the newspaper reported that the club, formed in 1902, was one of the oldest in West Herts (*WO* 23 October 1915).   That year the club had surpassed itself, winning county competitions for 50 and 25 yards. The mainstay of the club for years was its secretary and crack shot Mr A Beck.   The *Observer* commented that the club's past members now in the Army had also done well.  Recently, in the King's Royal Rifles (presumably the 16th Church Lads' Battalion), seven of the winning section were former Croxley Rifle Club members.

Meanwhile, the Croxley Green Company of the Church Lads' Brigade continued to be an important part of local life under Captain Jearrad, Lieutenant S Warn and Sergeant-Instructor Denton.   In January, the Dickinson Institute had organised a fund-raising event for uniforms for the Brigade members.   They attended regular church parades including one in Chorleywood on 28 November (WO 11 December 1915). With their bugle band, augmented by the band of the Watford Company, they marched there some 50 strong.   The Lads wore their new uniforms and were complimented for their smart appearance.

It wasn't just soldiers who were needed.   The curate at All Saints', Rev A G Backhouse, took a temporary assignment with the War Office in Lincolnshire (*All*

29. See Ian Beckett; *The Amateur Military Tradition: 1558-1945,* Manchester University Press, 1991, Chapter 8

*Croxley Rifle Club*

*Saints' Parish Magazine* July 1915 and *WO* 10 July 1915). His job was to superintend men who were harvesting hay and dispatching it to the front. In the September issue of the magazine he reported that he had obtained a motor cycle to make it easier to travel from one gang of men to another. As part of his job, he negotiated with farmers for the sale of hay ricks and commented that he was becoming an expert on the quality of hay. But the Bishop was keen that he should not escape his ecclesiastical duties entirely, so he was also taking Sunday services in a local church.

## Labour Relations at Croxley Mills

Dickinson's continued to suffer from the shortage of skilled labour. Unskilled workers, including many women, had to be employed. There was discontent over wages and working conditions. This is not surprising since inflation became a serious problem and undermined the value of wages during the war years. In 1915, the National Union of Paper Workers began recruiting in the Upper Mills (i.e. Apsley etc.). Initially, Dickinson's refused to deal with the Union. However, a strike was threatened at Croxley over late working on Saturdays and in July the Union held mass meetings to pressurise the company to improve wages and working conditions. According to Joan Evans, sensitive negotiation by the management avoided serious problems for the firm. Dickinson's provided bonuses for staff during the war period. At Easter 1916 staff received a bonus and double wages for a week in July and a gift at Christmas. Further bonuses were granted in September 1918.[30]

The paper, *War Time in a Paper Mill*, has little to say about war time labour relations beyond the statement that wages were from time to time amicably considered and very considerable advances were given.[31] Perhaps Barton-Smith did not want to

30. Evans, *The Endless Web*,
31. John Dickinson & Co. Ltd, *Croxley Mills, War Time in a Paper Mill 1914-18*, mimeo in local collection of Croxley Green Library.

enlarge on difficulties with staff.

## News from the Front

The war on the western front had become a stalemate with a steady stream of casualties. The Gallipoli landings in April failed to gain their objectives and the Central Powers completed a major victory over the Russians in May. The *Observer* attempted to maintain morale at home by reporting stories from local lads in the trenches. These included several Croxley men.

The Asprey brothers, David and Edward, had been Church Lads who enlisted early. They were serving in the 3rd London Field Company, Royal Engineers *(WO* 11 September 1915 quoting *ASPM)*. They had been chosen to accompany their Lieutenant, Denys Max Thomson Morland, on an attack on the German trenches. Morland was awarded the Military Cross for this exploit. According to the official announcement, he, 'on May 25th at Givenchy, accompanied a London Battalion in an assault on the German trenches, and finding the entrance of a mine, exploded it alone, making prisoners of eighteen Germans who were hiding in it'. Lt Morland and the Aspreys made it back safely. The Aspreys sent home as a souvenir a badge from a German helmet. They told their father that it had been a horrible crawl over many dead and wounded men when the officer spotted the helmet, and threw it to Edward as a souvenir. The helmet had been riddled with bullets, and as they were under heavy fire the young soldier cut the badge off.

*Private Henry Owen*

The March 1916 issue of *All Saints' Parish Magazine* reported that Corporal David Asprey, R E, had returned home after 13 months in France. Though he had been through all the big engagements, he had escaped without a scratch. The War Office had recalled him home to take charge of work requiring a skilled engineer. Then in September the magazine reported that Corporal Edward Asprey had arrived in hospital in Cheshire suffering from a damaged foot caused by a falling tree while in action. The Asprey family lived at 217 New Road.

The *Observer* reported the death on 9 August at Hooge in Flanders, of a prominent Rickmansworth man, Lieutenant Colin Taylor. James Wood Colin Taylor, 2nd Battalion Sherwood Foresters, was 28 when he died and is remembered on the Menin Gate at Ypres. One of the Croxley soldiers, Rifleman Charles Morris, 3rd Battalion Rifle Brigade, knew him. Morris wrote home that a few days before 9 August he saw Lt Taylor amongst his men and made up his mind that he would make an opportunity of speaking to him, but that never came. He added that Taylor's platoon all spoke with the highest respect of him. Morris commented that it was a dreadful sight after the

32

attack, but his unit had got the ground, and was holding on to it. They had just been relieved from the trenches after a fortnight's awful work, finding and burying the fallen. They had buried hundreds of Germans who had suffered terribly. The mine crater was full of them (*WO* 4 September 1915). In 1916, Rifleman Morris was recommended for the Distinguished Conduct Medal. His battalion suffered heavily from shellfire on Sunday 13 February. Morris did splendid work helping to remove many wounded to a place of safety (*All Saints' Parish Magazine* March 1916). He lived at 329 New Road.

Henry Owen joined up at the beginning of the war. His family lived at 147 New Road and he had served in the Herts Police at Hatfield. Private Owen joined the 2nd Battalion Grenadier Guards and was in France from August 1914. He was wounded at Ypres in November 1914. Then, almost a year later, his shoulder was hurt in a mine explosion just in front of the trenches (*WO* 23 October 1915). He had tried to get out of the way but was knocked down and buried before he could move. It was an awful sensation and it seemed as though he was under the earth for hours, being slowly crushed; however, he was making good progress in hospital.

The *Observer* and *All Saints' Parish Magazine* reported regularly on the growing numbers of wounded soldiers. Private James Hull of 36 New Road was hit in the thigh by a large piece of shell. The July magazine reported that he was making good progress and would soon be able to come home. Before the war he worked for Croxley Mills. Lance-Corporal Private Bert Chapman of the 3rd Dragoon Guards was wounded at Hooge and had to have his right leg amputated (*WO* 19 June 1915). He and his three brothers from 155 New Road, who had all volunteered early in the war, were celebrated in the Watford Illustrated of 11 January 1916. Bert subsequently had an artificial leg. *All Saints' Parish Magazine* commented in September 1916 how well he had recovered and hoped he would be as comfortable as possible with his new limb.

*Lance-Corporal Albert Chapman*

### Lieutenant Leslie Newall of Redheath killed

Second Lieutenant Leslie Newall, 1st Battalion, the London Regiment (Royal Fusiliers) was killed in Flanders on the night of 2 September. He was 23 and the eldest son of William and Lilian Newall of Redheath. His body is buried at Rue-David Military Cemetery, Fleurbaix, which is south of Armentieres, Pas-de-Calais, France. (According to the memorial in All Saints' church he was originally buried at Croix Marechal military cemetery, Fleurbaix. The grave was transferred after the war.)

The Newalls were an important family in Croxley Green and the surrounding area. They had come to live at Redheath in 1899. William was a member of the stock

*Redheath*

exchange and kept a substantial establishment (a governess and nine household servants in 1911). They had two other sons, Keith in the navy and Nigel in the army, and two daughters, Doreen and Gwynneth. William was born in Gateshead, County Durham, the son of a famous Scottish engineer, industrialist and amateur astronomer, Robert Newall.[32]

Leslie Newall was educated at Eton and Oxford, where he had just taken his degree in the summer of 1914. According to the *Observer*, he had applied for a commission as soon as war was declared and received it in August. In September he left for Malta with his regiment, which returned to England in February and left for Flanders on 10 March. On 2 September, he was out on patrol duty between the trenches when he was hit, became unconscious and died before he could be brought back. His Colonel wrote that he grieved not only at the loss of a good fearless officer, but for a personal friend who was loved by the men of the whole Battalion (*WO* 11 September 1915).

In October 1915 *All Saints' Parish Magazine* recorded that he had taken part in many severe engagements, in one of which a shell burst five yards away and buried him. He was dug out uninjured; a marvellous escape. The magazine's editor wrote that

32. See A M Clerke, 'Newall, Robert Stirling (1812-1889)', rev Anita McConnell, *ODNB*, OUP 2004.

Leslie Newall was not only a brave officer but a man of splendid character and lofty ideals. He died as he had lived, nobly and honourably. He was loved and respected by all who knew him, whether it was at home, or at school, or at college, or within his regiment. The editor offered sympathy to the Newall family and commented that the only consolation for the cutting short of a life so full of promise was the thought that however long he had lived he could do no greater thing than lay down his life for his friends. It was the ideal of all Christians.

An impressive memorial service was conducted by the vicar, Rev Edward Wells, assisted by the Rural Dean, Canon Parkinson, on 25 September (*WO* 2 October 1915). It attracted a large congregation, including some notable people: - Mr Frank Newall FRS (Professor of Astrophysics at Cambridge University) and his wife Margaret (a distinguished pianist), Sir James K Fowler KCVO (physician and academic) and Sir George Frampton RA (sculptor and craftsman).[33] At the conclusion of the service the bugle band of the 1/8th Sherwood Foresters sounded the 'Last Post'.

## The Church remembers

In the October edition of the church magazine the vicar, Edward Wells, struck a sombre note:

> The leaves have begun to fall, winter will soon be here, and the war still rages: indeed, unless something unforeseen occurs, there seems no prospect of peace for many months yet. But we must not lose heart. We must patiently endure this terrible cross and do all we possibly can to help and encourage our brave sailors and soldiers.

He went on to urge the parishioners to join regular prayer meetings. 'It is said that victory will be with the side which can last the longest in men and money and other essentials in war. But victory must depend largely, too, on the spirit of the nation; and what is it that can keep the spirit strong but faith in God…' (*All Saints' Parish Magazine* October 1915).

Monday 1 November was All Saints' Day and the dedication day of the parish church. Instead of the usual festival, a memorial service was held in the evening for the Croxley men who had died at the Front. There was a large gathering of relatives and friends and it was an emotional occasion as the vicar called on those present to remember those 'who had died gloriously in battle, giving their lives in the service of their country'. He listed eight names:

> Frederick Nathaniel Clarke, Robert Dooley, Frederick George Elbourne, John Henry Gardner, Leslie Newall, Arthur Toms, Frederick John Walker and Cecil George Wheeler. (*WO* 6 November 1915)

33. See the following entries in *Oxford Dictionary of National Biography*, OUP 2004: E A Milne, 'Newall, Hugh Frank (1857-1944), rev Roger Hutchins; R A Young, 'Fowler, Sir James Kingston (1852-1934)', rev Michael Bevan; and Tancred Borenius, 'Frampton, Sir George James (1860-1928)', rev Andrew Jezzard.

# THE BATTLE OF LOOS

By the middle of 1915, the Allies had assembled a large force to liberate the French territory taken by the Germans the year before. The French assaulted the southern part of the front in Champagne and their British allies attacked through the ruined mining villages and slag heaps of Loos and Lens, near the Belgian border. On the first day, 25 September, the British made significant gains, including the town of Loos. However, on the following days the attacking troops were sent into the teeth of German machine gun fire with disastrous results. Of nearly 10,000 British troops who attacked at Loos, 385 officers and 7,861 men were killed or wounded. The attack was renewed on 13 October but was equally unsuccessful and was called off due to bad weather and heavy casualties. (Martin Gilbert, *The First World War*, Weidefeld and Nicolson, 1994 p.201)

Several Croxley men were involved and four were killed.

 **Private Frederick Nathaniel Clark** of 3rd Battalion, Royal Fusiliers (City of London Regiment) was killed on 27 September (Loos memorial). His parents, Mr and Mrs Clark of Rose Lea, Croxley Green, placed a death notice in the *Observer* of 30 October, 'And so He giveth His beloved sleep'. Frederick was 25 when he died. In 1911, his father, Nathaniel, was an unemployed coachman and the family lived at 57 Pretoria Road, Watford. Frederick and one of his brothers worked as labourers in an iron foundry.

# CROXLEY MEN KILLED AT THE BATTLE OF LOOS

**Private Frederick George Elbourne** of 7th Battalion, Norfolk Regiment, had been one of the Chgurch Lads who enlisted early. He died on 13 October (Loos memorial). He was the eldest son of Joseph and Louisa Elizabeth Elbourne of 34 Scots Hill. He was born in Croxley on 2 April 1895 and baptised at All Saints' church. His father was a farm labourer and Frederick worked at Croxley Mills as a lad. He was the eldest of five children and only 20 when he died.

**Private Cecil George Wheeler** of 2nd Battalion, Bedfordshires was killed on 25 September (Loos memorial). He was 21 and the son of William and Ellen Wheeler of 8 Cassiobridge Terrace. The *Observer* of 30 October 1915 included a tribute by Corporal F A Roope. He wrote that they had orders to sustain the attack after the third line of German trenches was taken. They were advancing over open country when they were compelled to entrench. It was just before they started to dig trenches that Cecil was hit in the stomach. He was bandaged up straight away but it was too late. The Corporal commented that he died a hero doing his duty for his King and country and now lies in a hero's grave near to where he fell. The *Observer* added comments from a letter from Sergeant H Forder who wrote that Wheeler was as brave  as any man he had seen, always joking and cheering other fellows up when under fire. Private Wheeler belonged to the Special Reserve, and before the war, was employed by Mr Greeves, in his gardens at Scots Hill, Rickmansworth. According to the newspaper, Cecil's father was in France with the Royal Engineers and he had a brother in the army. In 1911 the Wheeler family lived in Belsize. Cecil, who was born in Wheathampstead, was the eldest of eight children. The family had also lived in Aldenham and Park Street.

**Private Albert Kempster** of 9th Battalion, Royal Fusiliers, died of wounds on 18 October and is buried in the cemetery at Vermelles, near Lens. He was born in Harefield on 6 September 1893, the son of George and Annie Kempster. His Croxley links appear slender but he was baptised at All Saints' church on 8 October 1893. In 1911, his mother, Annie, was a widow living with six children, including Albert, at 78 Norfolk Road, Rickmansworth. Albert was working as an engineer's labourer. After the war his wife, H A Kempster lived in Harlesden, London. [There are some discrepancies in the records. According to the Commonwealth War Graves Commission, he was 24 when he died but if the date of birth is correct he would have been 22. The written list in All Saints' church gives his first name as Alfred.]

The chancel was full of flowers. The service commenced with the hymn 'Fight the good fight', included prayers and hymns from the funeral service, and ended with the Church Lads' Brigade band playing the 'Last Post'.

## Croxley News

The *Observer's* edition of 30 October 1915 included an advertisement for Madame Tussaud's waxworks. They took pains to keep their exhibition up to date with war heroes including recent recipients of the Victoria Cross. Madame Tussaud's was of more than passing interest in Croxley because one of her great grandsons, John Tussaud, was living at the Hawthorns, 17 New Road.[34] In 1918 three of the family were serving in the armed forces: Bernard was a Second Lieutenant in the Machine Gun Corps, and Guy and Hugh were Lieutenants in the RAF.

Earlier in the year the junior members of the Dickinson Institute band had enjoyed their annual outing to the zoo and to the famous waxworks (*WO* 19 June 1915). Then on 6 November the *Observer* reported that a model of Nurse Cavell had been added to the collection. She was executed on 12 October 1915 by the Germans for helping Allied soldiers escape from Belgium.

## 16th Battalion, King's Royal Rifle Corps: Church Lads at the Front

As the year reached its end, the people of Croxley knew that the 16th Battalion King's Royal Rifle Corps was now in France after over a year in training. The Battalion, together with the rest of the 33rd Division, was reviewed by the Queen on 8 November soon before they embarked. The editor of *All Saints' magazine* wrote in the December edition:

> Definite news has reached us that the C L B Battalion King's Royal Rifles are now 'somewhere in France'. It is believed that they crossed the water early on the morning of Tuesday, November 16th. This means that thirty-five more Croxley men are at the Front. It need hardly be said that the movements of the Battalion will be in future a matter of keen interest and considerable anxiety to us all. One thing we know, that whatever they are called upon to do, they will do well. No finer body of men have ever set out to fight for their King and Country, and we can pay them no better tribute than that. We expect them to do great things, and feel certain that we shall not be disappointed. It is not very much that we can do for them now; but one thing we can do - we can pray that God may strengthen and protect them in all the many dangers they will have to face.

The 16th KRRC were first based in northern France. They marched to the Bethune area and from 4 December were gradually introduced to the trenches alongside more experienced troops. They remained in the trenches at Givenchy until 29 December when they were relieved, returned to Bethune and were able to enjoy a pantomime, Alladin, on New Year's Eve.[35]

34. Kelly's Directory 1913-14 and the 1918 Register of Electors.
35. Arthur Barton-Smith's diaries and George Horner, Church Lads' Brigade historical group.

Meanwhile, the local MP, Arnold Ward, received a big welcome in Watford as he returned on leave and toured the Conservative clubs with stories from the Herts Yeomanry in the Middle East.

*The Dickinson Institute hall arranged as a ward (1918 photo).*

## Voluntary Aid Detachment Hospital at the Dickinson Institute

Wounded soldiers had to be cared for and by November 1915 plans were well advanced to turn the Dickinson Institute into a Red Cross Voluntary Aid Detachment (VAD) Hospital with a capacity of 30 patients. However, according to *All Saints' Parish Magazine*, the beds had been held up in transit on the railways. Nonetheless, the Commandant, Mrs Kennedy, expected all to be in working order by the beginning of December.[36] Then, in its Christmas day edition, the *Observer* published a tribute to the work of all the local war hospitals, including those in Watford and Rickmansworth. They reported that the Croxley Green hospital was ready to receive patients. It would be attached to the Cambridge Eastern District Hospital. In due course, the Croxley Green hospital was linked to the County of Middlesex War

36. Mr and Mrs Charles and Florence Kennedy lived at Scots Hill House and Mr Kennedy was a JP (Kelly's Directory 1914-15 and 1918 register of electors)

Hospital which took over the premises of the Middlesex County Asylum at Napsbury between St. Albans and London Colney. Napsbury catered for 1,600 patients including a specialist mental hospital with 250 beds.[37] Wounded servicemen were first sent to Napsbury and, when they were well enough, they were moved to Red Cross hospitals such as the one at Croxley Green to convalesce.

The Institute's assembly hall had been converted into a ward and the Church Lads' Brigade club room into a mess room. The kitchen had been enlarged. There were three bathrooms and patients could make use of the Institute recreation room. If need be, the technical class-room could be converted into a second ward to bring the capacity up to 50 patients. Local residents had contributed £100 for the fitting out of the hospital and had given beds and other articles. Assisting Mrs Kennedy were Sister Nicholas (who had been for some time in an English hospital for French soldiers near the front line); Miss Barton-Smith, Quarter-Master, and Mr Barton-Smith Hon. Treasurer. All four continued in those capacities until the end of the war.[38] The hospital funds came from a grant of so much per man from the War Office plus subscriptions from local supporters (WO 25 December 1915). It is not clear when the first patients arrived but the Observer reported in its 6 May 1916 edition that a number of wounded soldiers from the Cambridge military hospital were quartered at the Institute.

Hosting the hospital meant that Croxley organisations had to find other venues for their activities. For example, the Girls' School, from 22 November 1915, started attending cookery lessons at Rickmansworth because they could no longer use the Institute. The girls also played an active role in supporting the hospital. The head mistress noted in the log book for 18 September 1916 that a large bundle of mending from the Red Cross hospital had arrived for the girls to sew.

Nonetheless, the seasonal rhythm of Croxley life continued. 'Neggy' Wilson convened the annual carol festival in the Girls' School which was very well attended. Mr Wilson gave a clever and convincing interpretation of what he termed the prevailing spirit of this particular coming Christmas, i.e. 'Comradeship'. The Church Choir and the organist Arthur Green rendered carols. There were solos by Mr H Lee, Mr W Chater, Mr H Toms, Jack Tandy and Frank Heckford and everyone joined enthusiastically in the carols (WO 18 December 1915).

---

37. See http://www.nationalarchives.gov.uk/hospitalrecords/details.asp?id=18&page=40 accessed 19 Nov 2013 and http://www.1914-1918.net/hospitals_uk.htm accessed 25 Feb 2014
38. The Barton-Smiths had three daughters May (c.1882 to 1948), Lilian (c.1884 to 1973) and Maud (c.1886 to 1972). Lilian was a professional nurse and May was the hospital Quartermaster.

*Croxley Green VAD hospital mess room.  May Barton-Smith foreground. (1918 photo)*

# 1916

The *Observer* opened the new year with a retrospective on 1915. Amongst the main local events the newspaper noted the training of the Croxley Church Lads as members of the King's Royal Rifles and the efforts by local people to support servicemen, including the Croxley Green Working Party which, with Miss Barker of Briery Close as President, did much good work in sending goods to the front.

However, Croxley's year began on a sad note because the first of the Croxley Church Lads in the 16th KRRC was killed, on 2 January.

---

## Death of John Victor Goodman

Sunday 2 January 1916 was a fateful day for the 16th KRRC when they took over the line in the Cuinchy sector, west of Lille and north of Lens. They rose at 4.30am and marched along the Bethune road and into the trenches. Almost immediately two or three mines exploded under them, the earth was blown into the air with a roar that could be heard miles away. Many were wounded or killed, the frantic digging of their friends released several of the men but others remained trapped in the trenches and dugouts. The ones who were found were buried in Woburn Abbey Cemetery, Cuinchy. The Germans followed up the mine blasts with heavy shellfire which caused the death of the first of the Croxley Lads, John Victor Goodman. According to *All Saints' Parish Magazine* of February 1916, John was killed instantaneously, aged only just 19; 'but he has died for his country and that is the greatest thing a man can do'. Harry Chapman was also wounded by the same shell and hospitalised in Eastbourne.(*WO* 15 January 1916) John is commemorated on the Loos memorial.

The Goodman family lived at 254 New Road. John's father, William, was a railway signalman. Both John and his brother, William, worked at Croxley Mills, although John is not listed on the Dickinson memorial.

---

Soon afterwards, the funeral took place of Jim Rogers, aged only 17 (*WO* 8 January 1916 and *All Saints' Parish Magazine* March 1916). He was the youngest of three sons of Mr and Mrs William Rogers of Dickinson Square. The next youngest, Charlie, was one of the Church Lads who had joined up in 1914 with the 16th KRRC and was then in France. Jim had previously met with an accident on the football field and, after some weeks' absence, had returned to work at Croxley Mills for a week, when he contracted an internal complaint from which he died in a few days. The funeral cortege to Rickmansworth cemetery was led by the Church Lads and the Croxley

Volunteer Training Corps. He had been a member of both and was remembered in All Saints' as a pleasant, good-natured boy, popular with old and young.

Nationally the news was not encouraging either. British and Empire forces had retreated from Gallipoli after a brutal and fruitless campaign and the Germans launched a huge offensive on the French lines at Verdun in February.

Arthur, Charles, Maud, Frank, May (snr) Barton-Smith

But not everything was gloomy. The Barton-Smith family were pleased that their second son, Frank, had gained a commission as Second Lieutenant and temporary First Lieutenant in the 1/12th Pioneer Battalion of the Loyal North Lancashire Regiment. He had been a member of the Inns of Court Officer Training Corps (*WO* 22 and 29 January 1916).

The local music teacher, Thomas Veale, made sure that his proteges received prominence in the *Observer*. Elsie Humphreys and Dorothy Raggett both passed the primary division of the music examination for the Royal Academy of Music and Royal College of Music. Elsie gained a distinction (*WO* 15 January 1916).

The war continued to make changes in the way of life. Daylight saving time was introduced in May 1916. The *Observer* reported on the scarcity of paper and a 40 per cent increase in its cost because of restrictions on imports. As a result the size of the newspaper was reduced from May. The schools were affected too. In compliance with the request of the Government that work should go on as usual at Whitsuntide and that the spirit of work should prevail throughout the country, Croxley Green schools did not close for the customary vacation (*WO* 17 June 1916).

### Conscription and the Military Service Tribunal

By the end of 1915 the British Government was increasingly concerned about how to gain more recruits for the Army. In the face of mounting casualties, the traditional voluntary approach to enlistment appeared inadequate. Conscription was totally against the principles of Prime Minister Asquith and his supporters in the Liberal Party, yet there appeared to be no alternative. After heated debate at Westminster, the Military Service Act of 27 January 1916 was passed and came into operation on 2 March 1916. To begin with, conscription applied to all British male residents aged

18 to 41 who were unmarried or a widower without dependent children. Married men were brought within the compass of the Act in June 1916. Then in 1918, as the need for recruits became ever more pressing, the age limit was raised to 50. Men had to undergo medical examinations to determine their fitness for war service. Early in the war these were rigorous but later the medical requirements were relaxed.[39]

The only way to avoid conscription legally was for individuals to apply to their local Military Service Tribunal. Exemption was possible on four grounds:
- ill health or infirmity;
- serious financial or domestic hardship;
- because the man concerned was engaged on work of national importance;
- conscientious objection to combatant service.

Urban Districts, such as Rickmansworth, were responsible for maintaining a local appeal tribunal. The panels were expected to be impartial, yet capable of having due regard for the national interest. The tribunal could dismiss an application or provide an exemption certificate that was absolute, conditional (for example on service in the special constabulary) or temporary. The tribunal's military representative could challenge the appellants and ask the tribunal to review previous exemptions. Appeals could be made to the Hertfordshire County Tribunal and, in exceptional cases, to a Central Tribunal.

The *Observer* reported in its edition of 12 February 1916 that the tribunals had been appointed in the previous week. To begin with, it was expected that they would complete their work in a few months but it turned out to be more difficult and protracted than expected. The County Appeal Tribunal heard its 3,000th case at the end of July 1917. The Chairman proudly stated that the 34 local tribunals in Hertfordshire had exempted only 11 per cent of all cases, compared with 20 per cent in Bedfordshire (*WO* 28 July 1917).

The Rickmansworth tribunal dealt with cases from Croxley Green and held its first meeting at the Council offices at the beginning of March 1916 (*WO* 4 March 1916). The chairman was Samuel Ingleby Oddie, a barrister and coroner for Westminster and south west London. He resided at Chess Side, Copthorne Road, Croxley Green and was active locally including as a member of the Urban District Council. There were two other Council members on the panel, both also from Croxley Green; James Coutts, who was Vice Chairman of the Council and William Catesby. Coutts lived at 3 Dickinson Square and was Clerk and Cashier at Croxley Mills. Catesby was a JP, lived at Highfield at the top of Scots Hill and was Chairman of Catesby's Ltd., General Furnishing Store, London. The other members were Alfred Norman Rickett (of Little Gillions Croxley Green), Newman Reynolds (a bootmaker living in Rickmansworth High Street), J R Mansfield (51 Church Lane, Mill End), Samuel Bateman, solicitor and later clerk to the UDC (Stafford House, Parsonage Road, Rickmansworth), and Donald Stewart (Batchworth House). The Clerk was H Lomas and the Military representative was C Ward Davey. The panel contained a strong element of local

---

39. Ivor Slocombe. "Recruitment into the Armed Forces during the First World War. The work of the Military Tribunals in Wiltshire, 1915-1918", *The Local Historian,* May 2000.

Conservatives.  Membership was fairly stable throughout the war.  Oddie was still chairman in 1918 when a further member of the Council, Philip Thornton, joined the panel.

Conscription led to much anxiety amongst families waiting to know whether their menfolk were going to be sent into the trenches.  Lizzie Toms wrote from Croxley to her son Edgar, who was training in Scotland, on 23 September 1916, 'There will be no men left about here soon. They keep going one after another. I do wish the fighting would end.' Edgar's uncle had initially been passed over on medical grounds but the family was on edge because he was recalled for re-assessment.

In November, the tribunal had to issue the following statement to clarify its role because of 'certain misapprehensions locally', presumably about the unfairness of the system.

> The Tribunal have nothing to do with calling up men for military service, but this is solely the duty of the Military Authorities.  The Tribunal have no means of knowing who is or who is not liable to serve.  It is a purely judicial body appointed to decide between the claims of the Military Authorities and the claims of the civil population to be exempted from serving in the Army in those cases only which come before them.  The Government Offices exempt many persons without any claims being brought before the Tribunals at all or without any notice to the Tribunals (*WO* 4 November 1916).

One of the largest local employers, Dickinson's Croxley Mills, did not bring cases to the Tribunal asking for exemption of their staff. In the early stages of the war they had encouraged men who could be spared to join up. They, presumably, also achieved what they wanted in terms of getting the government to exempt their essential personnel.  The *Observer* suggested as much when they reported on the tribunal case of a paper packer, George Wilcox, commenting that the military had granted exemption for men engaged at the mill (*WO* 28 July 1917).

At least 51 Croxley men applied for exemption, as reported by the *Observer*. The tribunal dismissed 19 of the applications and only gave 7 of them absolute exemptions.  Three of those absolute exemptions were rescinded in 1917 and 1918 as the shortage of men became ever more acute.  The 1918 absent voters' register and the list on All Saints' shrine, confirm that 27 of the men concerned did join up.[40] It appears that 11 did not and the outcome for the others is unknown.

Of course, not everyone obeyed the summons when the call-up papers came. In May 1916, one Croxley man, Charles Edward Kersley of 293 New Road, found himself before the local magistrates on a charge of failing to report (*WO* 27 May 1916). He claimed he had not received a notice but the Recruiting Office said they had sent two. A fine of 40 shillings (equivalent to 8 days wages for soldiers engaged in the 1916

40. The shrine in All Saints' church records those who enlisted in the armed forces from Croxley Green.  It is an important contemporary record but not complete.

harvest - *WO* 14 October 1916) was imposed and the defendant was handed over to the military authorities. In 1918 he was a Private in the 1/1st Cambridgeshires. By July 1916, the *Observer* contained lists of men who had failed to appear before the tribunals. At least two Croxley men fell in that category; George Rogers aged 36 of Dickinson Square and John Ingram aged 38 whose address was given care of the John Dickinson Paper Mill Boat (*WO* 29 July 1916). It is not clear whether either was tracked down.

## Frederick Randall killed

Private Frederick Randall, of the 8th Battalion, Bedfordshire Regiment, was killed on 19 April 1916. He is remembered on the Menin Gate at Ypres. In 1911 he, his wife and three small children lived at 266 New Road. He was 26. The family had arrived recently from London. Frederick worked as a gas stoker at the urban council works (presumably Rickmansworth). His widow, Alice, was left to bring up three young children: Frederick (9), Ada (7) and Edward (5).

### Keeping the economy going

The loss of men from the workforce created a lot of problems for employers and led to women taking a more prominent role in employment. By 1915 concern was being expressed about the impact of military recruitment on agriculture in West Hertfordshire. The Earl of Clarendon presided over a conference on war service for women in agriculture (*WO* 8 May 1915). Some felt that women could be no substitute for the young men who had joined up. Nonetheless, a West Herts Committee was established to recruit women for war service on the land (*WO* 15 May 1915). In 1915 the military gave leave for some troops to gain employment in the harvest. But that was not a sustainable solution in wartime and by May 1916 the *Observer* noted that the Women's National Land Service Corps was seeking recruits (*WO* 13 May 1916). The Hertfordshire War Agricultural Committee reported in October 1916 that 100 soldiers were used for the hay harvest and 250 for corn at the rate of 5 shillings per day. Some 2,000 women were engaged on field work wages of between 3 pence and 4 pence per hour. But the Committee noted that there still existed unreasoning prejudice against employing women (*WO* 14 October 1916). The issue surfaced at the Rickmansworth Military Service Tribunal which discussed the merits of women as milkers (*WO* 15 April 1916). It seems extraordinary today that they were debating whether women could substitute for men. However, resistance was widespread. The *Observer* quoted a local doctor on the subject. Doctors had tried to get exemption for their chauffeurs but tribunals had told them to use women drivers. One doctor claimed that women drove in a dangerous manner and it was too nerve-wracking to sit behind them (*WO* 5 August 1916).

*The Stationery Department at Croxley Mills in 1908. William Toms was the foreman. Private Plumridge (right) is bottom right in the photo above.*

Since Dickinson's had been so forward in encouraging their employees to enlist, they had to find a way of coping with the situation. The Chairman, Lewis Evans, speaking on 1 June 1916 at the Dickinson Institute, said that out of 278 men eligible for military service at Dickinson's [presumably from Croxley Mills rather than the whole company], no less than 241 had joined the forces (*WO* 3 June 1916). The remaining 37 were absolutely indispensable to keep the mill going. Nonetheless, total employment had actually increased from 724 hands to 805. This included a large number of veterans, women and boys. According to '*War Time in a Paper Mill*', the women mainly worked at paper sorting, waste paper pulping and the barking of timber. By the end of the war the mill was employing 410 women, compared to 224 before the war.

On 20 April, the company gave its staff an Easter bonus. The note from Lewis Evans recognised the willing spirit in which the staff had helped to keep the business going during the wartime difficulties. He hoped that the bonus would add to their enjoyment of a well-earned holiday. Croxley Green library has a document in its local collection which records the details of the bonus distribution and the way the company discriminated between its employees. The salaried employees and foremen received 20 shillings; married men 10 shillings; women, girls and single men 5 shillings and boys under 18 years of age 2 shillings and 6 pence. In April 1916, 798 people worked at Croxley Mills: 22 salaried employees, 17 foremen, 317 men, 333 women and girls, and 109 boys. The women and girls mostly dealt with the raw materials and the finished product while the men were concentrated in the mill itself, the boilers and repair shops.

During 1915 and 1916 the mill suffered a large increase in the cost of materials. Moreover, in March 1916 the Government restricted the import of papermaking materials to two-thirds of the quantity imported in 1914. Consequently, the management experimented with home production from a range of raw materials: flax waste, flax straw, peat, marsh hay, Norfolk reeds, bracken, nettles, oat and wheat straw. Following a severe storm in March 1916, which felled many trees, the mill management made plans to manufacture wood pulp. This began in August 1916 using a soda process and boiling the pulp in the esparto plant. With the help of this pulp and other home produced materials it proved possible to keep the whole of the seven paper machines running until the end of 1916.[41]

By the beginning of May, the VAD Hospital at the Dickinson Institute was in full operation. Lewis Evans and his wife inspected the hospital at the end of the month, after presenting long service medals to members of the Dickinson's Fire Brigade (*WO* 3 June 1916). During the presentation, the Deputy Chief Officer, L W Lovett, noted that the Fire Brigade, which was formed in 1883, had attended numerous outside fires in addition to outbreaks at the mill. The Brigade had also been very successful in competitions, winning twice the 'Blue Ribbon' of the Fire Service, plus numerous 2nd and 3rd prizes for fire drill and ambulance work. The following nine members of the Brigade were serving in the forces or the Red Cross: Corporal Eames, 5th Dragoon Guards, wounded in the retreat from Mons; Driver Dearman, Royal Horse Artillery, serving in France since the declaration of war; Orderly G Kerr, British Red Cross Society, serving in France since October 1914; Orderly E Warn, British Red Cross Society, serving in France since October 1914 (who had since rejoined the Brigade); Sergeant J Brackley, Gun Section, Bedfordshire Regiment, serving in France since October 1914; Sergeant Thurloe, East Surrey Regiment, wounded right arm; Assistant Farrier E Chapman, Royal Engineers, serving since September 1915; Private M Neale, Royal Berkshire Regiment (who subsequently was killed); Driver A Chapman, 3rd Dragoon Guards, who had his right leg amputated.[42]

## Fear of Air Raids

In the early days of the war, people had feared a German invasion and in 1914 the German Navy bombarded towns on the north east coast of England. Such fears may have subsided as the war became bogged down on the Western Front but there was

41. John Dickinson and Co, *War Time in a Paper Mill.*
42. All (except possibly Thurloe) were Croxley men. Neale was subsequently killed.

# THE BATTLE OF JUTLAND

In the early 1900s, it was the rapid growth of German sea power that most worried the British Government. Britain's economy depended on maritime trade and, for almost a hundred years, the Royal Navy had made sure that British trade routes were secure. By the outbreak of war the German High Seas Fleet had become a real threat. British naval commanders tried to lure the German Navy into a confrontation which they felt sure they would win. However, it was not until 31 May 1916 that the German High Seas Fleet ventured in force into the North Sea. The ensuing Battle of Jutland resulted in big losses for both sides. The Royal Navy lost more ships and men but the German High Seas Fleet was forced to retreat into harbour, where they remained for the rest of the war.

## THE DONNELL BROTHERS

**Lieutenant Ernest Tudor Donnell** died on 31 May 1916. He was second in command of HMS Shark, a destroyer in Admiral Beatty's squadron. Shark was heavily damaged but kept fighting on and sunk a German ship before being torpedoed. Shark's commander, Loftus Jones, won a posthumous Victoria Cross for his bravery. Only seven of the crew survived.
(http://www.royalnavalmuseum.org/info_sheets_loftusjonesvc.htm accessed 11 November 2013)

Ernest Donnell was the son of Rev Charles E Donnell, who was Croxley Green's vicar from 1899 to 1913. Charles Donnell moved to Stamfordham, Northumberland, just before the war so Ernest does not feature on Croxley Green's war memorials. Nonetheless, Ernest and his family would have been well known to many in the village. Rev Donnell returned to Croxley Green several times during the war and took part in the remembrance service in 1916. At the time, this must have been even more painful for him because another son, Arthur, had been badly injured and died soon afterwards.

**Lieutenant Arthur Patrick Donnell** of the Royal Flying Corps died in a flying accident on 5 December 1916 aged 18. He is buried in All Saints' churchyard, Narborough, Norfolk. Narborough was the site of a First World War airfield whose role was defence against Zeppelin raids. (http://www.raf.mod.uk/rafmarham/aboutus/narboroughaerodrome.cfm accessed 11 November 2013)

still the risk of attack from the air. The first Zeppelin raid was in January 1915 and, although the number of attacks was few, they received a lot of publicity and created much anxiety. These large airships were dramatic to see as they moved slowly overhead. There are no records of air raids in the Croxley area but All Saints' church took out insurance against air raid damage, which they increased to £1,000 in April 1917.[43]  In the autumn of 1916 the Germans launched a number of airship attacks on London with dramatic results in Hertfordshire. On 3 September 1916, airship SL-11 was the first to be shot down by a British fighter plane.[44]  Its wreckage landed at Cuffley, north of Enfield, causing much excitement and many sightseers. That was followed by the shooting down of L-31 on 1 October 1916 over Potters Bar. The fighter pilot responsible, Second Lieutenant Wulstan Tempest, has a road named after him in the town.[45] This was a boost to morale nationally and locally. William Toms, who lived in Yorke Road, wrote to his son Edgar who was posted to a training battalion in Scotland. 'I dare say you have seen in the papers the account of the bringing down of the Zep near us last Sunday night. I had the pleasure of seeing it from the window. I happened to be awake and saw the glare and then heard the tremendous cheering of the crowds in and around Watford. I think everybody in Watford, even if they had already gone to bed, turned out again that night.'[46]

### Rev Edward Wells

Edward Wells had been vicar of All Saints' since 1913.  He was increasingly concerned to support the men on the front line and responded to calls from the Young Men's Christian Association (YMCA) for voluntary help. The YMCA, along with other Christian organisations, had set up huts to provide some home comforts for the troops and to be a centre of Christian mission to soldiers. The *Observer* of 11 March reported that a fund-raising entertainment had taken place in the Girls' Schoolroom, Croxley Green, in aid of the soldiers' huts.

At the Easter Vestry meeting on 11 May 1916, Rev Wells told the church leadership that he planned to volunteer for several months at one of the YMCA's huts in France. He set off at the end of the month bound for Rouen (*All Saints' Parish Magazine* June 1916). The August magazine included a letter, dated 17 July, from him in France. His account gives the impression that life in the YMCA was somewhat humdrum. They were shorthanded and consequently he spent much of his time serving soldiers at the counter rather than getting to know them in any depth. By the time he was writing, the first stages of the Somme offensive had taken place and there were many casualties. He commented on the sad news that had reached him of three more Croxley men who had been killed in action. His own brother had been wounded again at the start of the battle.

The vicar returned to Croxley Green in September and his experience of three months

---

43. All Saints' Church Minute Book, 13 April 1917.
44. *WO* 9 September 1916, and Richard Van Emden and Steve Humphries, *All Quiet on the Home Front*, Headline Book Publishing, 2003, p.167.
45. See Potters Bar Zeppelin on Youtube and pbhistory.co.uk/war/zeppelin90.html viewed 23 May 2013
46. Letter from William Toms, 5 October 1916, from the family collection of Mrs Frow.

in France encouraged him to apply for a position as a military chaplain. He was accepted and resigned the living of Croxley Green on 10 December after barely four years (*All Saints' Parish Magazine* December 1916). Rev Wells wrote to his parishioners that he was eager to go and do what he could for the men at the Front, but the doctors had decided he was not fit enough to go abroad at the moment. Consequently, his first work in the Army was to be among the wounded at a hospital in London. He thanked the people of Croxley Green for their kindness during his ministry and asked for their prayers. He continued that, as a result of the war, with all its sorrows and anxieties, he felt they were all a little nearer to God. Many had discovered afresh the value of prayer to strengthen faith and deepen devotion.

*Rev Edward Wells in Chaplain's uniform*

One of his parishioners, Lizzie Toms, wrote to her son Edgar on 24 November, 'Mr Wells is leaving Croxley in a fortnight's time. I do feel sorry. He is going to be chaplain at a London Hospital where there are 800 wounded soldiers'. The vicar laid on a farewell social at the Vicarage for the Sunday School teachers and other church workers. Lizzie's husband, William, enjoyed dancing the Sir Roger de Coverley with Miss Barton-Smith. The girls from the Girls' School clubbed together to send the vicar an alarm clock, no doubt an essential piece of equipment in his new military calling.[47]

Edward Wells next appears on the local scene in December 1918 when he was instituted as vicar at St. James' Church, Watford Fields (*WO* 7 December 1918). According to the *Observer*, Rev E Wells came to St James as curate-in-charge in 1910, and after his time at Croxley Green had been out to France as hospital chaplain and YMCA worker. He was still obliged to continue with the forces for some three months after December 1918, until he could be properly released.

47. Croxley Green National School Log Book, January 1917.

The *Observer* reported regularly on the activities of the local regiments, the Bedfordshires and Hertfordshires, but in comparison with what was to come, the first half of the year was relatively quiet. Nevertheless, several Croxley men were wounded and one of the families affected was the Newalls. Lieutenant Nigel Newall, the youngest son of William Newall of Redheath, was seriously wounded and taken to a London hospital to recover (*All Saints' Parish Magazine* March 1916). His brother, Leslie, had been killed a few months earlier.

### 16th King's Royal Rifle Corps in France

After being blown up by German mines in January, the Battalion remained around the Givenchy area until July. On 11 January, Arthur Barton-Smith was sent out on a night working party. He jumped into a trench and broke his leg. As a result, he was evacuated to hospital in England. After convalescing he was passed as medically fit in May but then helped in the harvest before being drafted back to France in October.[48]

Some of the Croxley Lads, Jack Beament, Jack Brown, Herbert King and Charlie Rogers found a different way back to England. They arrived home in Croxley in good spirits on 15 February for some leave. No doubt Charlie would have been especially pleased to be home because he had married Miriam the previous July and it was an opportunity for him to support his parents after the death of his younger brother Jim. (*All Saints' Parish Magazine* March 1916 and *WO* 10 July 1915)

*Rifleman Arthur Hobbs*

While in the Givenchy area, the Battalion suffered over 100 casualties killed, wounded or missing, due to mines, shelling and sniping, as well as attacks on the enemy line.[49] Arthur Barton-Smith was in hospital at this time and mentions a number of his comrades as casualties in his diaries. Arthur Hobbs and Sidney King were both wounded.[50] Arthur Hobbs was hit in several places by shrapnel and was evacuated to hospital in Derby. Sidney was shot in the thigh by a revolver bullet which one of his comrades discharged accidentally. It caused a nasty compound fracture which was treated in hospital in Calais. Also Rifleman B Gunnell was shot through the shoulder and Cecil Gravestock received gunshot wounds to his right arm and right thigh.

Lance-Corporal Arthur Raggett was awarded the Military Medal for his bravery during the January fighting. The citation reads

48. Arthur Barton-Smith's diaries
49. George Horner, Church Lads' Brigade Historical Group.
50. Arthur Barton-Smith's diaries 27 February and 12 March 1916.

For conspicuously good work in charge of the stretcher bearers plus devotion to attending to the wounded during the fierce bombardments on 2nd Jan and again on the 28th Jan.[51]

---

# FRANK ARNOLD IS KILLED

On I July the Croxley Church Lads in the 16th KRRC were still on a northern sector of the front at Cuinchy, near Givenchy. It was here that **Rifleman Frank Arnold** was killed on 2 July, aged 20. On the night of 1-2 July, the battalion sent a party of 5 officers and 40 men across no-man's-land to raid the enemy trenches. Only 24 men made it back to the British lines that night. 5 men were killed including Frank, and his body was only recovered later under cover of darkness. (16 KRRC War Diary and Trevor Spinage)

 Frank, who was a labourer at Croxley Mills before the war, was the eldest of five sons of the Arnold family at 251 New Road. He is buried in Cambrin Military Cemetery, north of Lens.

---

## Tragedy at Cassiobridge

The *Observer* of 8 July reported on the death by drowning of George James Woods (aged 5). He was the son of Mrs Florence Woods and Private Joseph Woods of the 3rd Battalion Royal West Kent Regiment. The Woods family lived at 323 New Road with a lodger, Samuel Kerr. Mrs Woods and Mr Kerr went to the Halfway House by the canal at Cassiobridge with the four children on Sunday evening. They noticed George was missing about 9 pm. But it was not until the next morning that a policeman found his body floating in the canal. The Coroner said it was surprising that no one had noticed the deceased fall into the water as there were plenty of people on the spot at the time. He added that it might be advisable to keep a man at the place in order to warn people, and especially children, that the canal was dangerous.

## The 16th Battalion King's Royal Rifle Corps at the Somme

Such were the British casualties when the offensive began that Field Marshall Haig had to bring reinforcements from other sectors of the Front. The 33rd Division, including the 16th KRRC and the other three battalions of the 100th Brigade, was ordered south to join General Rawlinson's battered Fourth Army.[52] The battalion boarded trains at Lillers at midnight on 8-9 July. Their strength was 904: 27 officers and 877 other ranks. Next morning they were just east of Amiens and spent the next four days marching to Fricourt. On 12 July they rested at Morlancourt and, on parade

---

51. London Gazette, 3 June 1916 and 16 KRRC War Diary, 4 June 1916.
52. For this and what follows see Terry Norman, *The Hell They Called High Wood,* Patrick Stevens 1984, Lyn Macdonald, *Somme,* chapters 12 and 13 and 16th KRRC war diary.

*Troops going over the top on the Western Front*

# THE GREAT OFFENSIVE - THE SOMME 1916

As the New Army divisions reinforced the British forces on the Western Front, it became obvious that a big push by the Allies was planned to break the stalemate. By the early summer, the French, who had taken enormous casualties at Verdun, urged the British to lead an offensive further north and west. The front either side of the River Somme was chosen. Taking the British and French forces together, by June there were over half a million men ready for the offensive. The aim of the Allied commanders was to break through the well-defended German lines.

The initial assault took place on 1 July. The Germans were expecting the attack and the British bombardment had failed to neutralise the German artillery and machine guns. Consequently, the casualties on the first day were staggering and few of the British units made much headway. But the campaign continued with bitter and bloody fighting from July until November, when it petered out through exhaustion and bad weather. By the end of November, the British Army had pushed the Germans back about 5 miles but at the cost of over 420,000 casualties including almost 100,000 killed. The French and Germans suffered heavy casualties too. British newspapers, including the *Observer*, carried long lists of the dead, wounded and missing. Almost every community in the country was affected and the scale of the casualties began to undermine optimism at home. Croxley Green lost 10 men killed and suffered many wounded.

# CROXLEY GREEN MEN KILLED AT THE SOMME 1916
## Charles Strugnell

Second Lieutenant Charles Strugnell died on 1 July 1916, the first day of the Somme attacks. He had only just been promoted from Trumpet-Major in the 16th (Queen's) Lancers into the 2nd Battalion, (Princess of Wales') Yorkshire Regiment. The 2nd Yorkshires were regular soldiers, part of the 21st Brigade and 30th Division. They attacked towards Montauban but were soon halted by machine gun fire and suffered 200 casualties. (Ray Westlake , *Tracing British Battalions on the Somme*, 1994.) According to his commanding officer, Strugnell was killed while bravely leading his men. He is remembered on the memorial to the missing of the Somme at Thiepval.

Charles Strugnell had been a member of the Church Lads' Brigade. He was unusual because he was a professional soldier and came from a family with a history of military service in the Yorkshires. His grandfather served in the regiment. His father, Charles senior, joined the regimental band as soon as he was old enough, attended the Royal Military School of Music at Kneller Hall, and became bandmaster to the Yorkshires. When he retired from the army as a Warrant Officer, Charles senior came to work for Dickinson's and became bandmaster of the Dickinson Institute band. The family lived at 245 New Road.

Charles junior was the only son and attended Watford Grammar School for Boys, unlike most of his peers in Croxley who ended their education at the Boys' School in Watford Road. He decided early on to follow in his father's footsteps and by 1911, aged 22, was already a Lance-Corporal musician in the 16th Lancers. His death must have been a severe blow to the family, probably not helped much by the letter from his Colonel expressing deep regret at the loss of so gallant and promising an officer.

(*WO*, 24 June and 15 July 1916, *All Saints' magazine* September 1916.)

that day Cecil Gravestock made what the army referred to as an 'improper remark'. Unfortunately for him, he was overheard by an officer and found himself on a charge. He was given 28 days field punishment number one, which meant loss of pay, going to the bottom of the leave rota, and being handcuffed to the wheel of a gun carriage for two hours every day.[53]

The rolling chalk countryside north of the river Somme forms gently sloping cornfields interspersed with woods and small villages. As they arrived near the front line, it would have seemed familiar to Croxley men from the edge of the Chilterns. The Germans had dug their fortifications on the ridges and the Allied armies were fighting uphill amongst woodlands that provided excellent cover for German machine-guns.

Despite the generally disastrous outcome of the British attack on 1 July, there had been some successes in the south, near Montauban alongside the French. Rawlinson planned to follow this up on 14 July with a major assault on the second line of German defences between Mametz wood and Trones wood. The aim was to dislodge the Germans from the ridge about a mile and a half to the north. High Wood (Bois des Fourcaux) is on the crest of the ridge. Learning from the mistakes made on 1 July, Rawlinson planned to surprise the enemy by assembling his troops in darkness and beginning the attack before dawn. In anticipation of victory, he prepared the 2nd Indian Cavalry Division to punch through the German lines and press home the advantage. The initial attack by six brigades of the Fourth Army (about 20,000 men) was remarkably successful and the British troops managed to push their way up the slope. Vigorous pursuit of the retreating Germans might have captured High Wood itself during the morning. But it was not until the afternoon that tired detachments of the 1st South Staffordshires and the 2nd Queen's entered the wood. By then the Germans had recovered enough to put up some stiff resistance. The cavalry had to pick their way through the shell holes and destruction behind the new British front line and it was late when they arrived on the scene. By then the advantage had dissipated and they were easily repulsed. Nevertheless, the British Generals judged it had been a successful day with German losses higher than the 9,000 casualties suffered by the British. Would it be possible to sustain this hard-won progress the next day?

The 16th KRRC, with their colleagues in 100th Brigade (1st Queen's, 9th (Glasgow) Highland Light Infantry and 2nd Worcesters), moved up to Fricourt, while the attack was in progress. Jack Beament and Jack Brown described the journey to Lyn Macdonald.[54] It was a hot day and something of an endurance test as they marched with full kit. They had to pass through the original British front line. There were still bodies unburied from the fighting two weeks before and the road was flanked with heaps of overturned waggons, broken equipment and dead horses. The smell was terrible.

On 14 July, the men stood to at 3.45 am and, after breakfast, they were issued with picks and shovels, extra rounds of ammunition and two sandbags each. Thus

53. Cecil Gravestock's military records transcribed by Trevor Spinage.
54. Lyn Macdonald, *Somme*, p. 140

*High Wood from the Contalmaison to Longueval road.*
*'B', 'C' and 'D' Companies 16th KRRC attacked from right to left across the slope from the track beyond the hedgerow.*

burdened they marched up the steep-sided valley towards Mametz wood where the Welsh Divisions had suffered so many casualties a week before. They reached their assembly positions just beyond Mametz wood late in the evening and proceeded to dig themselves in.

The 100th Brigade had received orders to attack the next German line of defence, the Switch Line, which cut through the far corner of High Wood, at 9 am the next morning, 15 July. The 1st Queen's and 9th Highlanders were to lead the attack with the 16th KRRC and 2nd Worcesters in support. See sketch map, page 59.

That night the 1st Queen's took cover in the lane leading from Bazentin-le-Petit to High Wood while the 9th (Glasgow) Highland Light Infantry crossed the open ground in the darkness to secure the nearest corner of High Wood. They met enemy fire. Unknown to them, the Germans had reinforced the Switch Line and around 11.30 pm a strong German counter attack drove most of the British troops out of the wood. The Highlanders began digging in by the lane on the edge of the trees. Men of the 16th KRRC carried up ammunition, bombs, water, picks and shovels to 1st Queens' and the Glaswegians. 'A' Company 16th KRRC, under Major Cooban, was sent up to support the Highlanders. Nobody got much sleep that night, especially Brigadier Baird, in charge of 100th Brigade. He now knew that the Germans still controlled most of High Wood. They would be in a perfect position to enfilade his men with machine-gun bullets from the flank if the attack went ahead the following day. He tried to get the orders changed at divisional headquarters so that High Wood could be captured first but was rebuffed. The attack was to proceed as planned.

'B', 'C' and 'D' companies moved off about 7 am. It was a misty morning. They passed the conspicuous crucifix at the head of the lane from Bazentin-le-Grand and found

*Crucifix corner*

their assembly points in the track just beyond, leading up towards High Wood. Some 1,200 yards to the north were the 1st Queen's, assembled in the lane from Bazentin-le-Petit, with the Highlanders near the wood on their right. Their objective, the German Switch Line, was another 700 yards beyond the furthest British positions and out of sight. Fearing a disaster, the Brigadier ordered A company to join a company of the Highlanders to force the Germans out of the wood.

The attack was preceded by an artillery bombardment from 8.30 am which proved ineffective. The mist lifted and the sun shone. At 9 am the attack began and, immediately, the attacking troops were met with a hail of bullets from High Wood and the Switch Line. The Highlanders suffered terrible casualties. 1st Queen's managed to reach the barbed wire in front of the German trench but they were forced to retire. Companies 'B' and 'C' of the 16th KRRC followed and as they gained the top of the slope near the wood, they found themselves amongst dead and dying Scots. Soon the machine-guns were trained on them and they suffered the same fate.

'A' Company fared even worse with the Highlanders in High Wood. From the moment they entered the trees they were met by a hail of bullets and grenades. They battled on, taking what cover they could, until they came to a small clearing. In the clearing the Germans had built a concrete blockhouse containing two or three machine guns. Very few made it back out of the wood. 'D' company was sent to reinforce them but they were beaten back quickly and could only dig in along the wood's southern edge.

Jack Brown and Jack Beament were both in A Company and gave a graphic account of their experience to Lyn Macdonald.[55] Beament was a stretcher bearer. The attacking troops only managed to get twenty or thirty yards into the wood before they were forced to take whatever cover they could find in shell holes. Jack Brown was hit in the back and Beament got a bullet in his left shoulder. With difficulty, Brown jettisoned his kit, crawled to the edge of the wood and stumbled back down the lane to a forward dressing station. Jack Beament was crawling out when he encountered another wounded KRRC man, Johnny Redman. Beament dragged him out with him and carried him back to the dressing station. The two Jacks managed to walk back, suffering from loss of blood, down the valley away from the carnage to get their wounds dressed.

55. Lynn Macdonald, Somme pp. 146-150

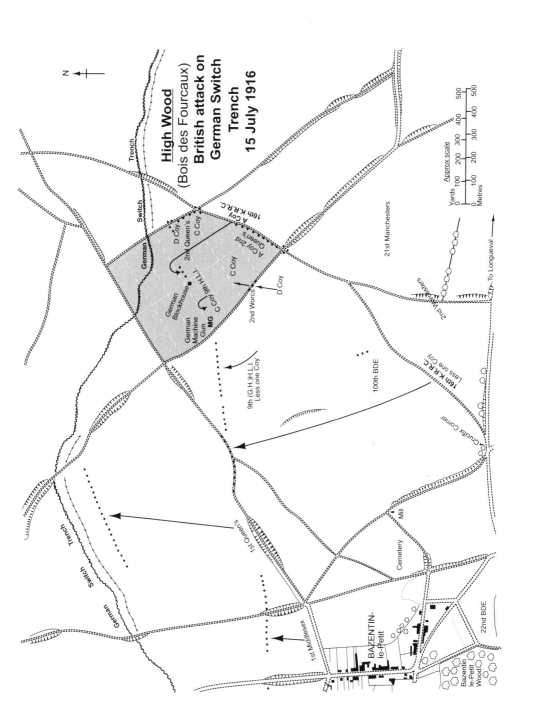

High Wood
(Bois des Fourcaux)
British attack on
German Switch
Trench
15 July 1916

N

Trench

German
Switch

Switch
Trench

German
Trench

D Coy
2nd Queen's
C Coy
A Coy
16th K.R.R.C.
A Coy 2nd
Queen's
9th H.L.I.
German Blockhouse
C Coy
MG
German Machine Gun
C Coy
2nd Worcs
D Coy

9th (G.H.)H.L.I.
Less one Coy

100th BDE

16th K.R.R.C.
Less one Coy

21st Manchesters

2nd Manchesters

To Longueval

Crucifix Corner

1st Queen's

Mill

Cemetery

1st Middlesex

BAZENTIN-
le-Petit

Bazentin
le-Petit
Wood

22nd BDE

Approx scale

Yards    0   100   200   300   400   500
Metres   0   100   200   300   400   500

Jack Beament summed it up as a 'horrible, terrible massacre'. 'A' company had over 200 men when it entered the wood that morning. Only 67 came out. Major Cooban had been killed. The other officers had been either killed or wounded, as had all the sergeants and all the corporals. The most senior man who now took charge of the remnants of the company was Croxley's Herbert King, lance corporal of two weeks standing.

That day 100th Brigade suffered terrible casualties: 59 officers and 1,308 men killed, wounded or missing. Of the four battalions, the 16th KRRC had suffered the most - over 60 per cent casualties. From the Croxley Church Lads, Cecil Gravestock was killed. Charlie Rogers was reported as wounded and missing. Wilfred Warn died a few days later of his wounds.

Besides Jack Beament and Jack Brown other wounded Croxley men included Tom Brown, Ben and Bert Gunnell, John Gudgin and Arthur Howard (*WO* 22 and 29 July and 12 August 1916). Jack Beament was eventually taken to a base hospital in Rouen. By an amazing coincidence, amongst the thousands of casualties, he found himself in the same ward as his younger brother Stanley who had also been wounded in the shoulder. Stanley was in the 20th (Pioneer) battalion of the KRRC and, unknown to Jack, he had been consolidating the trenches close to High Wood on 14 July when he was hit.

John Gudgin had been badly wounded and was taken to hospital in Leeds. Initially it seemed he would not pull through but he recovered and was medically discharged from the army on 30 June 1917. Subsequently, he appears as a bugler teaching youngsters in the Church Lads' Brigade and at remembrance events in Croxley. Three other Croxley Lads were medically discharged because of their wounds: Bert Gunnell (28 February 1917), Frank Sills (24 August 1917) and Arthur Howard (3 May 1919).[56]

The battle for High Wood continued for another two months before the wood, by now reduced to a mess of twisted and charred tree stumps, finally fell to the British. Only then was the body of Charlie Rogers found.

Ten days after the massacre at High Wood, Herbert King was promoted to full corporal; he transferred to the Royal Engineers the following year. Jack Beament was awarded the Military Medal for bravery in the field and he too was eventually promoted to corporal.

On 30 December 1916 the *Observer* commented that of the 35 Croxley Church Lads who enlisted in the 16th KRRC at the beginning of the war only 6 or 7 were currently in the front line because the others had been killed or wounded. This is hard to verify because comprehensive records of those wounded are not available. Certainly five were dead. Appendix 1 charts the situation of the group as a whole during the war.

56. Information from Trevor Spinage, based on records of silver war badge.

# CROXLEY GREEN MEN KILLED AT THE SOMME 1916 - 2

**16th Battalion King's Royal Rifle Corps at High Wood**

**Rifleman Cecil Gravestock** was killed outright during the attack on 15 July aged 20. Cecil was the second of three sons of George and Emma Gravestock of 321 New Road, born in Croxley on 26 May 1896. Like Frank Arnold, Cecil worked at Croxley Mills and they were both very young. *All Saints' Parish Magazine* commented that it was only seven years since they were both playing together in the school football team. Cecil is remembered on the memorial to the missing of the Somme at Thiepval.

**Rifleman Charlie Rogers** was also killed on 15 July aged 25. He was a wheel wright by profession and, unusually amongst the Croxley Lads, he was married. He left a grieving young widow, Miriam (nee Hudson). His parents, William and Grace of 7 Dickinson Square, had already lost their youngest son, Jim, earlier in 1916 as the result of an accident. Charlie is buried in Caterpillar Valley Cemetery, Longueval, just across the fields from High Wood.

**Lance-Corporal Wilfred Warn** died of his wounds a few days later (22 July) aged 28. His parents, Thomas and Elizabeth lived at 222 New Road. Wilfred worked in the grocery store of Croxley Green Co-operative Society. He was rejected three times by doctors when he tried to enlist in the early days of the war but persisted until he found a doctor willing to pass him. *All Saints' Parish Magazine* (September 1916) paid tribute to Wilfred's fine character, and commented that he was in every way a splendid comrade and soldier. Probate for Wilfred's estate was granted to his eldest brother Sidney on 24 January 1917. He left £140.8s.10d.

*Looking towards High Wood from Caterpillar Valley cemetery where Charlie Rogers is buried*

## CROXLEY GREEN MEN KILLED AT THE SOMME
## 1916 - 3

The military details in this box and boxes 4 and 5 are based on Ray Westlake, *Tracing British Battalions on the Somme*, 1994.

**Private Walter E Element** of the 13th Battalion, Middlesex Regiment, was killed by a shell on 18 August while carrying machine gun ammunition. The battalion (73rd Brigade, 24th Division) took part in an attack towards Guillemont that day. Walter was initially reported missing and was not officially presumed killed until July 1917 (*WO* 14 July 1917). He was 19 years and 11 months old when he died. Walter's father Henry was a boot maker and the large family (11 children) lived at 119 New Road. Walter helped in the business and is listed on the Dickinson memorial. (Thiepval Memorial.)

# CROXLEY GREEN MEN KILLED AT THE SOMME
# 1916 - 4

**Private Maurice Neale** of the 6th Battalion Royal Berkshire Regiment died of wounds on 7 October and is buried at Rouen. The 6th Royal Berkshires (53rd Brigade, 18th Division) had seen action since July at Montauban, Delville Wood and Thiepval and had suffered serious losses. Neale was 31, the son of William and Elizabeth Neale of Watford, husband of Mary Neale of 18 Sydney Road, Watford and father of Edmund and Maureen (*WO* 9 October 1920). He is listed on the All Saints' Shrine as having joined up in 1916. In 1911 Maurice was living with his mother, then a widow and mother of nine surviving children, at 12 Grosvenor Rd., Watford. His mother was born in Berkshire. Maurice's occupation in 1911 was a house decorator but, in the *Observer* of 3 June 1916, he was recorded on the roll of honour of Dickinson's Fire Brigade. The *Watford and West Herts Post* of 10 October confirms that he was a member of the Croxley Mills Fire Brigade and a watchman at the mill.

**Sergeant William Goodman** of 7th Battalion, Norfolk Regiment died on 16 October just short of his 22nd birthday, and is buried at the Guards Cemetery, Lesbeoufs, Somme. The battalion (35th Brigade, 12th Division) was involved in an attack on German trenches near Gueudecourt on 12th October. They were faced with heavy machine gun fire and uncut barbed wire. Casualties were heavy and they were forced to withdraw. Like his brother John, who was killed in January, William worked at Croxley Mills, was a member of the Church Lads' Brigade and was one of the first from Croxley Green to join up. He was born in Croxley on 1 November 1894 to William and Sarah Goodman who lived at 254 New Road. They had three children, William, John and Kate. William senior, was a railway signalman. *All Saints' Parish Magazine* in December 1916 commented about the

family that the death of their other son had made this fresh sorrow doubly hard to bear. William had been a chorister at All Saints'. He had seen a great deal of fighting and had distinguished himself, winning the Military Medal and attaining the rank of Sergeant. The editor continued that he was always so cheerful, so unselfish and so good tempered. 'He was a loyal churchman who had made the greatest sacrifice and was an example to us all. We shall not forget him.'

# CROXLEY GREEN MEN KILLED AT THE SOMME 1916 - 5

**Private Frederick Groom** B Company, 11th Battalion, Royal Sussex Regiment, (116th Brigade, 39th Division) died on 3 November aged about 21 and is buried at Rouen which was a hospital centre for treating British casualties. On 3 September the battalion succeeded in entering the enemy's front line near Hamel and then on 21 October they took part in the capture of Stuff Redoubt near Thiepval. The fighting was heavy and each time they suffered almost 300 casualties (about a third of the battalion's strength). Frederick joined up in 1914. His parents, Robert and Sarah Groom, and their two sons lived at 3 Yorke Rd. Both Frederick and his father worked at Croxley Mills although Frederick is not listed on the Dickinson memorial.

**Lance-Corporal Frank Hobbs** of 7th Battalion, Bedfordshires (54th Brigade, 18th Division) died on 16 November aged 23. At the end of September the battalion attacked Thiepval and the enemy defences at Schwaben Redoubt. They were based near Ovillers when Frank Hobbs was killed. He was born in Croxley on 19 August 1893, the son of Thomas and Martha Hobbs. In 1911 the family lived at 86 New Road. They were another Croxley Mills family. Frank's father, Thomas, was an engine driver at the mill and both he and his brother, Arthur, were labourers there. Frank was also a chorister at All Saints'. (Thiepval memorial.)

**Private James Lyons** 13th Battalion Rifle Brigade (111th Brigade, 37th Division) died 14 November aged 23. On that day, the battalion was attached to 63rd (Royal

Naval) Division and successfully attacked Beaucourt trench. James Lyons was born in Croxley on 11 November 1893. He was one of the Croxley Church Lads who enlisted at the outset of hostilities and joined the 16th KRRC. In 1911 the Lyons family lived at 14 Dickinson Square and in 1918 they were still in the square at number 22. James' father, James senior, was a papermaker at Croxley Mills and he and Rose Lyons had seven children. James senior and Rose were both Croxley born and married on 24 December 1891 at All Saints'. James junior was a fitter's apprentice at the mill (but he is not listed on the Dickinson memorial) and a chorister at All Saints'. (Thiepval memorial.)

*Thiepval Memorial to the Missing of the Somme*

# DEATH OF GUNNER LEONARD PITKIN

**Gunner Leonard Pitkin** died in Yorkshire while training on 3 September 1916 aged 33. He slipped, was run over by the wheel of a gun carriage and died shortly afterwards. Leonard belonged to the 27th Anti-Aircraft Company of the Royal Garrison Artillery. In 1911 he worked as a clerk at Croxley Mills and lived with his father George, a Dickinson's pensioner, at 9 Dickinson Square. Leonard's father had been a beater-man at the mill and his mother was Charlotte. The family came from Apsley. His death was completely unexpected and came as a great shock to his family and friends since he was not thought to be in danger. William Toms wrote to his son Edgar, 'You will be sorry to hear poor Len Pitkin is dead. He met with an accident.... He was engaged with an anti-aircraft section at a quiet little village near Leeds. They were moving their gun and he tried to mount whilst the carriage was in motion, slipped and fell under the hind wheels....and died very quickly. Poor quiet Len is gone.' According to the vicar at All Saints' (in the October 1916 magazine), Leonard was a reserved man, a faithful member of the church and teacher in the Sunday School. 'His steadfastness in this and other similar labours will not be forgotten, nor go unrewarded.' He is buried in Chorleywood Road cemetery, Rickmansworth.

*The Pitkin family grave*

At least the Pitkin family could bury Leonard in the family grave. That was not an option for the other grieving families because the government had decided in 1915 not to repatriate any of the fallen. In many cases, soldiers were blown to pieces or rendered unrecognisable so there was no body to bury. Of the 10 Croxley men killed at the Somme in 1916, five have no known grave. It was a cold process.[57] The army sent a formal letter to tell the family that their loved one was killed or missing. Generally, his platoon officer would also write with a little more detail, usually emphasising the dead soldier's bravery and popularity with his colleagues. But families were given little real idea of how or where he died.

The emotional impact on grieving relatives and friends must have been complicated by the government's decision to make a propaganda film about the Battle of the Somme, which includes a sequence of British soldiers 'going over the top'. It was shown for a week in October 1916 at the Electric Coliseum in St Albans Road, Watford, while the fighting was still going on.

The *Observer* reported surprisingly little on events at Croxley Mills, apart from a number of tragic accidents there. One particularly unpleasant incident occurred on Saturday 9 September. Mrs Eliza George of 27 Cardiff Rd Watford was engaged in some work which necessitated her stooping, when her hair caught in part of the machinery and the whole of the skin was torn from her head. First aid was rendered by some of the employees at the mill and Dr Evans was summoned. Mrs George was taken to the the district hospital, where, according to the paper, despite the shocking nature of her injuries, she was recovering (*WO* 16 September 1916).

## Conscientious objection and the Military Service Tribunal

In the circumstances of such bloodshed at the Somme, it is hardly surprising that those who sought exemption from military service on conscientious grounds should be vilified as 'shirkers'. The *Observer* reported one case from Croxley Green: Arthur Sidney Prime, who came before the tribunal in October 1916. He displayed considerable courage, because 'C Os' or 'conchies' were seen by many people as

57. See Van Emden and Humphries, *All Quiet on the Home Front*, chapter 4.

unpatriotic and cowardly traitors. The editor of the *Observer* concurred with this view. He drew attention to the chairman of the Berkhamsted tribunal, Major Parsons, who said that if anyone was doing God's work it was the man who was killing Germans. The editor commented that it was a strange sort of religion which called on its adherents to stand aside 'in maudlin contemplation' while their fellow Englishmen were freely shedding their blood 'in the struggle against the most barbarous form of militarism the world has ever known'. In his view the highest ideals of Christianity were being acted out by those going forth 'cheerfully against the Huns' (*WO* 4 March 1916).

Prime was 32, lived in Yorke Road, and was formerly employed by John Dickinson's as a papermaker's machineman. He said that war was anti-Christian and he claimed the privileges of the Toleration Act under which men were given the liberty of serving God according to their conscientious belief.[58] Prime had been a member of the Plymouth Brethren but was now a Seventh Day Adventist. He had resigned his employment with Dickinson's because working on Saturday was against Adventist beliefs. Prime said that he felt bound to offer to do non-combatant service. This set him apart from the more extreme conscientious objectors who were not prepared to accept any form of conscription or war service. The tribunal gave Prime exemption until 30 November so he would have time to join the Non-Combatant Corps which had been set up in March 1916 as part of the army. Members of the Corps were army privates, wore army uniform and were subject to army discipline, but did not carry weapons or take part in battle. Their duties were mainly physical labour in support of the military, including acting as stretcher-bearers and medical orderlies.[59]  It is not clear what happened next but Prime appeared again before the tribunal in May 1918 and was, again, ordered to join the Non-Combatant Corps. It may be that he avoided conscription altogether. According to the 1918 electoral register, he and his wife Beatrice were living at 'Rosemary', Yorke Road.

## Domestic hardship and the Military Service Tribunal

Given the imperative of finding more recruits for the Army, the tribunal gave short shrift to those applying for exemption because of their domestic circumstances. Even two of Croxley Green's influential households failed to get their way. Edward J Graver, butler to the Newall family of Redheath, was only allowed one month's grace before joining up and Miss Dugdale, of Croxley Grove, failed to convince the tribunal to exempt her chauffeur and groom, Joshua Guise (35) of Tudor Cottage. Again, he was only allowed a month. In 1918, both Graver and Guise served in the Motor Transport Companies of the Army Service Corps

58. 1689 act of Parliament granting freedom of worship to Nonconformists. *Encyclopaedia Britannica Online Library Edition.* Retrieved 10 May 2013 from http://library.eb.co.uk/eb/article-9072799
59. See Peace Pledge Union www.ppu.org.uk/learn/infodocs/cos/ and The Long Long Trail www.1914-1918.net/labour.htm

C B Bird, aged 38 of 120 New Road, was a motor driver for John Dickinson's. He said that he had served 12 years in the forces and did not want to serve any more. It would be very hard for his wife, who suffered from ill health, if he was called up. The tribunal gave him 6 months' exemption in June 1916. In January 1917 he had failed to turn up for his next hearing but, by then, he had joined the Red Cross as a driver. Another Croxley man, Alf Warn of 107 New Road, joined the Red Cross and was given exemption from service in the armed forces so long as he continued to work for them.

The Chapman family of 155 New Road were locally celebrated because four brothers had joined up early in the war and one, Bert Chapman of the 3rd Dragoon Guards was seriously wounded in 1915 and had had his leg amputated. So, when their younger brother, eighteen-year old G Chapman, was called up, his father sought his exemption in July 1916 saying that he had eight sons alive of whom five were serving in the forces. The tribunal was initially sympathetic and gave six months' exemption but by January 1917 they had changed their view and G Chapman was forced to enlist. He was subsequently wounded.[60]

## Remembering the dead

*Rev Charles Donnell as a young man*

The vicar, Rev Wells, was very conscious of how inadequate it all was for those who had lost loved ones. He wrote in the October 1916 *All Saints' Parish Magazine*, 'While sadly writing these meagre details of men who have lived and died so nobly, one wishes that it were possible to write more fully and adequately of each one...'. He tried to strike a positive note, 'These men have passed on, but the memory of what they have done remains and will remain. We shall never forget. It is hardly possible to give expression to the deep sympathy we feel for the relations of those who have been taken, but we pray that God will comfort them in their sorrow.'

Formal commemoration at the church was the nearest that the families could get to a traditional

60. See entry on All Saints' shrine

funeral. As in 1915, All Saints' church used All Souls Day at the beginning of November to remember the Croxley men who had died. There was a large attendance and the previous vicar, Rev. Charles E Donnell, took part. It must have been particularly poignant for him, since he had lost one son at the Battle of Jutland and another was, at the time, severely wounded. He had been well liked as vicar of All Saints' and Lizzie Toms wrote that it was good to see him but he had aged ten years in the three years since leaving Croxley. 'He is much thinner and very grey. Of course, the trouble of losing his son and having another badly wounded would help to change him.'[61] The Donnells' second son died on 5 December 1916. Like other Croxley mothers with a son in the army, Lizzie Toms worried about the war and could not face the idea of attending the memorial service. She wrote to her son Edgar, 'Dad and Douglas are going but I don't know if I shall yet, sometimes I feel I shall be best away.'[62]

The vicar read out the names of 17 Croxley men who 'had died gloriously in battle, giving their lives in the service of their country':

> Frank Arnold, Frederick Clarke, Robert Duly, Frederick Elbourne, John Gardner, John Goodman, Cecil Gravestock, Maurice Neale, Leslie Newall, Leonard Pitkin, Frederick Randall, Charles Rogers, Charles Strugnell, Arthur Toms, John Walker, Wilfrid Warn and Cecil Wheeler.

The service was a solemn affair which included the Psalm, 'The Lord is my Shepherd', the Russian memorial hymn and the National Anthem. The Church Lads' Brigade sounded the 'Last post' (*WO* 11 November 1916). A month later, as Edward Wells preached his farewell sermon to the congregation at All Saints', the choir sang the 'Contakion of the Faithful Departed' in memory of three former choir boys who had died: William Goodman, Frank Hobbs and James Lyons.

### The *Observer* bolsters morale.

The *Observer*'s editor, who had been such a strong supporter of the war, could not ignore the pain inflicted on families throughout the district as casualty numbers increased. He used his editorials to try to keep up morale. In August, on the second anniversary of the outbreak of hostilities, he commended the way the district had risen to the demands of the war, assured his readers that victory was in sight and urged them to remain determined to carry on to the end (*WO* 5 August 1916). He singled out the patriotic records of the local private and grammar schools whose staff and pupils had joined up in large numbers. He encouraged schools to keep a record of their old boys in the forces so that fitting memorials could be prepared for the honoured dead and gallant living.

---

61. Letter from Lizzie Toms, 9 November 1916.
62. Letter from Lizzie Toms, 2 November 1916

Again, in November he commented with pride, and regret, on the record of the local regiments, the Hertfordshires and Bedfordshires, which, judging by the casualty lists, had borne their full share in the fighting (*WO* 25 November 1916). That week's losses in the ranks of the Bedfordshires alone occupied over a column of the *Observer*'s space. He noted that many brave lads from the district had laid down their lives since the great offensive began, and their names would go down to posterity on the already long roll of honour. He hoped that the new recruits who would fill the gaps would soon acquire the same determination as their veteran comrades to hold on to the last gasp and to die rather than let the Regiment down.

It is not clear how such sentiments were received in Croxley Green. One suspects that many people just tried to get on with their lives. The *Observer* provided a window on the more prosaic aspects of life too. It reported the 114th quarterly meeting of the Croxley Co-operative Society which took place on Thursday 26 October (*WO* 4 November 1916). Under the guidance of the president, Mr E Irwin, and secretary, Mr J W Page, the normal business was soon concluded. But this meeting was a bit out of the ordinary. The management of the Croxley Green society had decided to erect a memorial tablet to George W P Taylor, the Society's secretary for 17 years, who died on 2 May 1916, aged 46 years. They had invited pioneers and 'spade workers' of the society of 25 and 30 years ago to be present. Among these were Mr Coutts,[63] its first secretary, president and auditor, Mr Heckford, an early secretary and long time co-auditor, and Mr W Lack president for many years. The memorial was erected in the shop and placed in front of it was a roll of honour which mentioned one employee, Wilfred Warn, who had died and two others who were serving in the war.

As the year drew to a close, the people of Croxley could reflect on the way the war was having a greater impact on the village. 295 men had enlisted by the end of 1916 and 23 had died.[64] Many had been wounded, although there are no reliable numbers. Combing through the long casualty lists for Croxley names is not easy. Nonetheless, the *Observer* recorded the following: - Harry Chapman, William Webb, Jack Beament, Tom Brown, Ben Gunnell, Bert Gunnell, Arthur Howard, John Gudgin, (all of the 16th KRRC); Stanley Beament (19th KRRC), S W Newberry (Royal Field Artillery, wounded in the head, hand and arm), H Lamsley (Grenadier Guards); and Lance-Corporal F Gray, in civilian life popularly known as the 'Colonel' (Hertfordshire Regiment).

The *Observer* commented that the record of the old Croxley Church Lads' Brigade members, who joined the KRR, was especially notable. The newspaper listed soldiers from the district who had won medals for bravery, including four Croxley

63. One of Croxley Green's prominent citizens. James Coutts was Cashier of Croxley Mill and a member of the Rickmansworth Urban District Council. He lived at 3 Dickinson Square.
64. All Saints' shrine

men: Distinguished Conduct Medal for Charles Morris, Rifle Brigade; Military Medals for Lance-Corporal Arthur Raggett and Private Jack Beament of the 16th KRRC, and for Sergeant William Goodman, Norfolk Regiment, who had since been killed.[65]

In his review of 1916 the *Observer*'s editor drew attention to the prodigious voluntary work for the comfort of soldiers at the front and for the care of the wounded and bereaved (*WO* 30 December 1916). The district had also contributed substantial funds for the war effort. Business was carrying on but with a much depleted work force. Nonetheless, he admitted that, for many, 1916 had been a terrible year. It had brought sorrow, pain and tears. However, he hoped that, as a result, the end of the struggle for freedom was well within sight, some time in 1917.

Christmas in Croxley provided a welcome relief from such cares and an opportunity for family gatherings. Like other families, the Toms made the best of it without their eldest son, Edgar, who was posted to a training battalion in Scotland. Edgar's youngest brother, Douglas (aged 9), wrote to Edgar afterwards to thank him for sending some toffees. He took pleasure in listing his Christmas presents, including slippers, several handkerchiefs, a flashlight bulb, some magic lantern slides and chocolates. He also commented, 'In our playground before the holidays there were the best slides you ever seen. They were so good that Negie [Wilson], slid on them and he can't half. He had about 50 slides and only went down twice. You should see him. When he went down the boys did laugh.' The Toms family knew Neggy Wilson well both from school and from his role in leading the church choir. He came round to see them from time to time. On 10 January 1917 Lizzie Toms wrote that he had dropped in the previous Sunday evening. She asked him, 'to play a carol just to finish the day up. He did and we all sang so you know that we made a good noise but that was a good finish to Christmas'.[66]

---

65. The DCM was the equivalent award for gallantry for non-commissioned soldiers to the Distinguished Service Order for officers. The DCM ranked ahead of the MM which was the non-commissioned equivalent of the Military Cross. http://www.greatwar.co.uk/medals/ww1-gallantry-awards.htm accessed 7 December 2013.
66. Letter from Lizzie Toms, 10 January 1917

*'Neggy' Wilson and pupils, Croxley Boys' School, early 1900s*

# 1917

## Munitions work

Keeping the army supplied with ammunition was a constant concern and a munitions worker's wages were attractive. Several Croxley people went to work in the industry. In January 1917, Cyril Toms (aged 16) and a friend, Bert Lyons, volunteered for munitions work in London. Both were from Croxley Mills' families. Bert's older brothers, James and Tom, had joined the Church Lads' Battalion and James had been killed the previous November. Initially Cyril took digs in London, which must have been expensive, but later he commuted from home on the early 'workers' train'. Munitions work was dangerous. On 19 January 1917 there was an enormous explosion which destroyed a TNT factory at Silvertown in East London: 73 were killed and 300 injured and between 60,000 and 70,000 neighbouring properties were damaged.[67] Cyril's mother Lizzie Toms wrote to her older son Edgar , 'What do you think about the explosion. It was at Silvertown. We heard it here. I went down to Mrs Darvill's to tea. Dad called for me on the way home and stayed to tea. We were sitting talking and the door shook ever so much. We all wondered what had happened but we did not know until the next morning. Poor old Cyril heard it very plain. He is working in Grays Inn Road'.[68] The following month Lizzie wrote, 'There was an explosion at the munitions factory in Watford on Tuesday. I think there has been four deaths and several injured. The people had to clear out of their homes and get right away and the L O school children had too. They came this way'.[69] In March there was a fire at Cyril's works and a girl was killed.[70] A week later, Lizzie wrote to say that Cyril was at home because the workers were out on strike. They went back a week later.

Frederick Cyster, of Yorke Road and subsequently Dickinson Avenue, was a chemist at Croxley Mills. His father, Frederick John Cyster, of 211 New Road, was a carpenter who worked for Dickinson's as well as for local builders. Frederick junior enlisted in

67. See Museum of London - museumoflondon.org.uk/Collections-Research/Research/Your-Research/X20L/timeline/silvertown.htm - accessed 31 July 2013
68. Letter from Lizzie Toms, 25 January 1917
69. Letter from Lizzie Toms, 15 February 1917. The munition factories were located in Bushey Mill Lane and Imperial Way, North Watford. Fire broke out in one of them on 13 February 1917. Two women were burned to death and several were injured. J B Nunn,*The Book of Watford*, 1987 p.137. The L O school is the London Orphanage later known as Reed's.
70. W. Cubitt & Co., Gray's Inn Road.

the Royal Engineers in 1916 but was recalled from the Western Front to work on improving cordite for explosives. The government developed an enormous munitions complex on the coast of the Solway Firth stretching from Annan in Scotland almost to Carlisle. H M Munitions Factory Gretna commenced production of cordite in August 1916.[71] Frederick worked there and the family were billeted in Annan for much of the time from 1916 to 1918. As it happened, his wife's family, the Galleys, were also involved in supplying the military. Thomas Critchfield Galley and sons made leather bandoliers, leggings, belts and other goods for soldiers and sailors at his leather works in Parkside, Rickmansworth and at Mill End.[72] Two of his sons, Fred and Alf Galley, lived in Croxley. They both enlisted and ended the war as air mechanics in the RAF.[73]

## Hungry times

*Frederick Cyster*

By the spring of 1917, Britain faced serious food shortages. The poorest families experienced real hunger and some areas suffered food riots.[74] Home food production had been restricted by the war's demands for men and horses, but the main problem was the lack of supplies from overseas. Two-thirds of Britain's food (measured in calories) was imported. In the early years of the war Germany had restrained its submarine attacks on merchant ships to avoid bringing America into the war. But in February 1917, the Germans launched a major onslaught on Britain's seaborne lifeline. In April, U boats sank 373 ships bound for British ports, about a quarter of the total shipping tonnage. From February, enormous quantities of meat and grain en route for Britain were destroyed. The government was slow to respond but, as the year went on, the introduction of shipping convoys meant that more supplies got through.

The *Observer's* coverage of these issues was patchy and it is not clear how many local people suffered extreme hardship. Thanks to employment at the mill and their closeness to local farms, Croxley people probably fared better, on the whole, than those, for example, in the East End of London. Nonetheless, everyone had to make do with less and there was real anxiety about when the food, especially wheat, would run out.

The correspondence between the Toms family of Yorke Road and their son Edgar in the army gives us some insight into the situation locally. The family took a lot of

71. See Gordon L. Routledge, *Gretna's Secret War,* Bookcase 1999.
72. See Alan Priest, *Rickmansworth Historical Society Newsletter*, Number 79 and Adrienne and Christopher Jacques, *Rickmansworth a Pictorial History*, (Phillimore, 1996) photo 97.
73. Personal communication from Judy Priest
74. See Van Emden and Humphries, *All Quiet on the Home Front*, pp 189-219

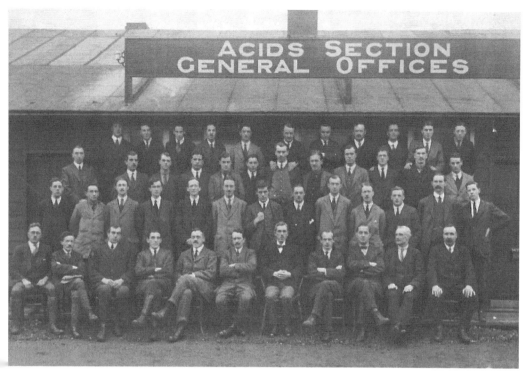

*Fred Cyster and managerial colleagues at H M Munitions Factory Gretna. (This photo gives a misleading impression of the workforce. There were over 20,000 workers and most of them were female.)*

trouble to make sure that Edgar received regular parcels of food and tobacco from home. By 1917, however, supplies were beginning to run short for the family in Croxley Green. Edgar's mother, Lizzie, reported in February 1917 that there was 'talk of cutting the bread ration' and she could only get a few potatoes at a time. She added that Edgar's father, William, was trying to get a piece of ground to grow potatoes on.[75] William applied to a local farmer, Mr Stone, and was successful. Getting enough coal was a problem too. Lizzie wanted to bake some cakes to send to Edgar but she wrote, 'We are so short of coal, I am afraid to use it to get the oven hot enough to cook much. We are on our last scuttleful but we are hoping to get one bag up tomorrow to go on with'.[76] On 30 March she reported that Edgar's Aunt Nellie had been without coal and sugar. In reply, Edgar joked from his training camp in Scotland, 'if you are short of coal, we have about half a hundredweight in our room here which probably we shall not use. So if you would like it just send me a wire and I will send it through the post, but please state whether you will have it all at once or a lump at a time'.[77] Things must have improved at home because Nellie did manage to send Edgar some cakes for Easter. But potatoes were still an issue. In April, Edgar's Aunt Edie Jackson wrote to him, 'There seems a great difficulty in getting potatoes everywhere. How do you get on? We are fortunate to have our own. I am allowed 10 a day and then [Uncle]

75. Letter from Lizzie Toms, 28 February 1917. Rationing was not compulsory until 1918.
76. Letter from Lizzie Toms, 23 March 1917
77. Letter from Edgar Toms, 27 March 1917

Ern says we shall have enough to last until they come again.......How do you like the war bread? I can't get on with it myself but the others like it. I suppose we shall have to keep on smiling in spite of it all'.[78]   Stories of the privations at home were not easy for the troops to deal with. Edgar wrote in February 1918, 'We hear terrible rumours out here occasionally of the shortage of things in Blighty'.[79]

The government launched a food-saving campaign in the spring of 1917 and, at the beginning of May, Lord Clarendon appealed to everyone to conserve the stock of wheat by cutting back on the consumption of bread, preventing the waste of other foodstuffs and leaving the cheaper foods for the poor (*WO* 5 May 1917).   The government was very reluctant to introduce rationing because, as with conscription, it went against Liberal principles.

Nonetheless, by June the situation was so grave that there was no choice but to exert more control on the production and distribution of food.   Local authorities were required to take steps to ensure that food was not wasted.   Rickmansworth Urban District Council appointed a surveyor and assistant inspectors under the Food Control Act. Their work was intrusive.   For example, the *Observer* reported that the surveyor had inspected 240 dustbins for waste of bread and had warned several shopkeepers who were charging more than the price fixed (*WO* 16 June 1917).   Charles Barton-Smith was elected to deal with any food control cases (*WO* 14 July 1917).   Judging by the columns of the *Observer*, prosecutions under the Food Acts seem to have been rare.   However, prosecutions did take place.   A resident of Berkhamsted was fined under the Sugar (Domestic Preserving) Order for obtaining sugar under false pretences and not using it for preserves (*WO* 10 November 1917).

A flagrant case of hoarding in nearby Commonwood came to light early in 1918. William Edward Allen of Commonwood House, Chipperfield, was charged before Watford Magistrates with a breach of the Food Hoarding Order (*WO* 23 March 1918). There were 18 summonses relating respectively to:
> 183 lbs tea, 134 lbs sugar, 352 lbs bacon, 56 lbs cocoa, 60½ lbs biscuits, 144 lbs Quaker oats, 52 lbs Scotch porridge oats, 229 lbs oatmeal, 297 lbs rice, 96 lbs pearl barley, 31 lbs macaroni, 41½ lbs lentils, 32 lbs gelatine, 98 lbs Lyle's syrup, 23 tins of condensed milk, 174 packets of turtle cup food, 19 bottles essence of chicken, and 352 lbs jam.

The Watford Rural Food Committee had received a complaint and their Inspector had obtained a warrant and searched the house.   Mrs Allen had laid up a 'war store' in 1915 because of her fear of a German invasion.   The Ministry of Food Inspector had visited in 1917 and declared himself content.   There were twelve members of the household.   The food hoarding order forbade anybody to acquire any foodstuff in excess of the quantity required for ordinary use. The Watford Magistrates concluded that it was perfectly clear that in this case considerable quantities had been acquired since the Inspector's visit.   Therefore they convicted the defendant, fined him £350 plus costs and confiscated 90% of the goods.   However, Mr Allen appealed to the

78. Letter from Edie Jackson,15 April 1917. Grain such as maize and barley and potatoes were added to bread to make the imported wheat go further.
79. Letter from Edgar Toms,14 February 1918

Hertfordshire Quarter Sessions where the fine was considerably reduced, although excess food was forfeited (*WO* 13 April 1918).

John Dickinson and Co used flour in their industrial processes and in June 1918 they were charged with taking delivery of flour contrary to the Bread (Prices) Order 1917 and with using flour, contrary to the order, to make paste (*WO* 29 June 1918). However, Dickinson's were exonerated in court. Their suppliers (Bailey's, millers, of Watford) had understood, incorrectly, that the flour did not come under the measure because it had been recovered from the hold of a torpedoed ship and so was not fit for human consumption. A licence was issued retrospectively.

Food Control Committees were established in Rickmansworth and Watford in September. The Rickmansworth committee was chaired by Croxley's James Coutts, who was also chairman of the Council. The members comprised three others from the UDC, W E Catesby, W J Murray and P Thornton; two lady members, Mrs Hay of Tolpits and Miss E Bristow (Girls' School); two labour members, A Payne, Grove Road, Mill End and W Turner, 88 New Road, Croxley Green; and three others, S A Bateman, W A Carr and the Rev F Halsey (vicar of Rickmansworth) (*WO* 29 December 1917).

The Watford committee reported on the food situation at the beginning of October (*WO* 6 October 1917). Meat prices had been fixed. Flour stocks were enumerated. There were particular problems in obtaining sugar, and tea was scarce. In the same issue, the Observer published a letter from a farmer who complained that government had set the price for potatoes at £6 when he would have been willing to accept £5! The *Observer's* leader on 3 November 1917 dealt with the work of the Food Control Committees and commented in particular on the inconsistencies in the system. For example, the price set for milk in Watford was 8d a quart but only 6d in Rickmansworth. Enforcement must have been a problem but in May 1918 at least one malefactor, Winifred Mayer, was convicted at the police court for selling milk at 7d instead of 6d per quart. She was fined 10s for each of eight summonses plus 14s costs (*WO* 1 June 1918).

In July 1917, the *Observer* struck a lighter note as it covered the good cherry harvests in Croxley Green and the neighbouring districts of Rickmansworth (*WO* 21 July 1917). The paper reported that the fruit was dispatched daily to the London markets. Visitors flocked to the orchards for three consecutive Sundays, known as 'Cherry Sundays', during the harvesting to taste this delicious fruit.

From the middle of 1917, the government took steps to boost arable production, especially wheat, barley and potatoes. Hertfordshire War Agricultural Committee was set up to implement the policy. By March 1918 the committee had instructed farmers to plough and crop 12,800 acres previously used for other things (*WO* 30 March 1918). Persuasion was not always enough as the case of Lady Ela Russell of Chorleywood House demonstrated (*WO* 16 March 1918). She was found guilty at Watford Police Court of failing to obey an order to cultivate land under the Defence of the Realm Regulations. Lady Russell said that she was producing butter and meat on the land and was helping the food production of the country better than by

*Members of the Women's Land Army*

ploughing up the land for an uncertain wheat crop. Moreover, she had no men to do the work. William Banting of Redheath Farm, Croxley Green, was a member of the inspection committee for the parliamentary division of West Herts. He said that he was a practical farmer, farming 300 acres and, after inspecting the land, he agreed that it was in the national interest to plough it up. Others disputed the land's value for arable. The Magistrates imposed a fine of £100. Chorleywood Urban District Council felt that this was monstrous and it would be disastrous to Chorleywood to have the dairy closed.

Labour shortages were a continuing issue. In March 1918, the *Observer* reported that farmers had applied for soldier labour and the War Office had made arrangements for prisoners of war to work for farmers (*WO* 30 March 1918). By May 1918 there were 40 POWs working on a farm in Rickmansworth (*WO* 18 May 1918).

In January 1918 the Women's Land Army was officially launched. The *Observer* of 25 May 1918 reported on a procession of land workers, organised to promote the Herts recruitment campaign. The procession assembled outside the Red House, Croxley Green, and paraded to Mill End, stopping on Croxley Green, Johnson's Corner, the Recreation Ground, and Mill End Post Office. The procession, headed by the Caledonian Pipers, and comprising decorated farm carts and farm implements, had the enthusiastic support of local farmers, several of whom were included in the parade. Mr R S V Ayre, Mill End, acted as marshal. According to the reporter, the local land girl workers turned out in strength looking very fit and sun-

# DEATHS OF WILLIAM WOOLLAMS AND WILLIAM CARTER

**13 March Private William Arthur Woollams** died of wounds. He is buried at Lijssenthoek Military Cemetery, near Poperinghe, Belgium, alongside almost 10,000 others. Lijssenthoek village was the location of casualty clearing stations for soldiers fighting on the front line near Ypres. Rifleman Woollams served in the 6th Battalion (City of London) Rifles, London Regiment. He was 22 when he died. He and his parents, Joseph and Mary Rose Woollams lived at 231 New Road. William, like his father, was born in Croxley Green and worked at Croxley Mills. He was a cutter. In 1911 he had five brothers and a sister.

**14 March Private William Carter** died. He is buried at Heilly Station Cemetery, Mericourt-L'Abbe, between Albert and Amiens in the Somme area. Casualty clearing stations were located here during this period. Private Carter served in the 1st Battalion (Duke of Cambridge's Own) Middlesex Regiment. He was born in Croxley on 13 June 1891 to Charles and Emma Carter. He was 24 when he died and his mother was living at 46 Scots Hill. In 1911, Emma was already a widow. William had four siblings and worked at Croxley Mills as a paper mill hand. In 1911, one brother and one sister also worked there.

tanned. At each stopping place, the recruiters appealed for women land workers.

In spite of all this activity, food shortages were still a problem at the end of 1917. Queues were commonplace. In Watford, margarine was in short supply (butter was very hard to come by) until a special effort was made to improve distribution at the end of the year (*WO* 29 December 1917). The *Observer's* editor approved of proposals by the Food Controller to end the 'queue scandal'. He complained in late December that, nearly every day, long lines of men, women and children were to be seen in the High Street patiently waiting for hours to get into certain shops. The pavements were blocked and tempers were frayed over the waste of time and frequent disappointments (*WO* 22 December 1917).

The government decided to introduce rationing for certain commodities from January 1918 and the Observer approved (*WO* 19 January 1918). Soon afterwards, the meat shortage in West Herts led to meat rationing in Watford (*WO* 9 Feburary 1918).

However, for those with money, there were always better options. In October 1917 the International Stores predicted a shortage of tea but recommended coffee for breakfast instead. Then in March 1918, the Empress Restaurant in Watford High Street reassured its customers that they could continue to rely on choice food with excellent service in spite of the food restrictions. Fruit jellies and fruit salads were one of their great attractions.

## Conscription and Farming in Croxley Green

Against the background of inadequate food supplies, the Rickmansworth Military Service Tribunal found itself deciding between local farmers wanting to hang on to their workers and the army desperate for new recruits. The tribunal dealt with seventeen cases from Croxley Green involving farming, including five from the watercress industry. Their conclusions varied from case to case but, generally, although they were sympathetic to farmers trying to keep their businesses going, agricultural labourers were required to enlist.

James Dorrofield was 40 in 1916 and lived at Fishery Cottage (and subsequently the Pest House) in the Chess valley. The *Observer* of 6 January 1917 records that he owned 4 acres of cress, 2 of potatoes and 20 of hay. Dorrofield appeared before the tribunal six times between June 1916 and October 1918. Each time he was granted a temporary exemption to continue the business and in December 1917 he was also required to join the Hertfordshire Volunteers. On his final appearance before the tribunal in October 1918, Dorrofield handed in a certificate establishing that his occupation was protected by the Board of Agriculture and Fisheries. However, James' younger brother Joseph Dorrofield (aged 35 of 1 Yorke Road) had his application for exemption refused in June 1916. Joseph went on to serve as a Private in the 1/5th Royal West Kents.

The Sansom family also grew watercress locally. In March 1916, one of their labourers, William Treacher (118 New Road) was exempted for two months to gather in the watercress harvest. He enlisted later in 1916 and served as a Gunner with the Royal Field Artillery. Charles Herbert Sansom (aged 29 in 1916) had taken over his parents' business at Croxley Hall. According to the *Observer*, he farmed 30 acres (including 10 acres of market garden and 8 of cress) in Hertfordshire plus 7 acres in Hampshire (*WO* 24 March 1917). In March 1916 he was granted 6 months' exemption on the grounds of serious financial hardship. Then in June he appeared before the tribunal again and they adjourned his case pending further instructions (presumably from the War Agricultural Committee). Charles applied for exemption for one of his watercress cutters, Daniel Ward (aged 36 of 1 Vine Cottages, Scots Hill) in November 1916. Sansom argued that he had already cut back his work force to nine men and two boys compared to fifteen before the war. However, the application was dismissed and Ward joined up. In 1918 Ward served as a Private in the 729th Labour Company. Charles himself faced the tribunal again in March 1917 when the Military Representative challenged his exemption.

Meanwhile, Charles' uncle Harry (Henry George) Sansom ran his watercress business at Cassiobridge. In January 1917 Harry (40) was granted 6 months conditional exemption but then the Military Representative applied for a review in May. According to the report in the *Observer* of 19 May 1917, Harry had offered to look after his nephew's business while he joined the Army, but his nephew had produced a medical certificate saying that he was tubercular and thus unfit for military service. In his defence, Harry Sansom said that he had eight children, the eldest in the army and the youngest in the cradle. His conditional exemption was renewed provided he joined the special constabulary. At about the same time as this was going on in Rickmansworth, Harry's eldest son Frederick was killed in action in France. Neither Charles nor Harry enlisted. Charles went on to become the first chairman of the National Watercress Growers' Association in 1928.[80]

Despite the importance of agriculture in the war effort, farm workers did not always receive preferential treatment. Alfred Gunnell (271 New Road) was a market gardener and watercress cutter. He also argued that his parents were both elderly and he was their sole support now that two of his three brothers were in the army. Gunnell was refused exemption and enlisted in 1916. George T Snelgrove of Scots Hill Cottage was also refused in June 1916 in spite of arguing that he was a farmer and market gardener. In 1918, Snelgrove was in the 131st Labour Company.

Age and the difficulty of replacing skills appear to have been factors in the tribunal's decisions. Ernest Hart (39) of 149 New Road was a ploughman working for John Coxhill of Killingdown Farm. He was granted conditional exemption in June 1916. A year later, the case of Harry Richard Sear (42), farmer and fruit grower of Scots Hill, was adjourned for instructions from the War Agricultural Committee. In 1918 he was registered as still living in Scots Hill so it seems that he was exempted. Coxhill, who is recorded as farming 50 acres, also applied for exemption for a cowman, Herbert Parsons (30 of Little Green), in November 1916. Parsons was a member of the Volunteer Training Corps and Coxhill described him as absolutely indispensable. He too was granted conditional exemption.

Walter Stone was less successful. According to the *Observer* of 4 November 1916 he had five cows and 15 young stock and was a contractor for the County Council. The tribunal dismissed applications for two of his sons, Jesse Walter Stone, cowman and coal carter and G W Stone (29) carter, contractor and cowman. Both enlisted and the 1918 election register records Jesse Stone as a Private in the 19th Middlesex Pioneers.

By 1918 the pressure to enlist was becoming greater, especially for younger men. Two agricultural cases from Croxley reached the County Appeal Tribunal. W T Dickins was an eighteen-year old cowman on the family farm at Croxley Hall. In December 1917, he was given a final exemption until March 1918 which he appealed unsuccessfully. Another eighteen-year old, William Spencer Banting, worked for his father at Redheath farm as both a horse ploughman and a motor tractor driver. Mr W Banting senior (47) emphasised that he had adopted modern farming techniques by becoming the first man in the county to buy a motor tractor. Mr Crawford, for the appellant, argued strongly for exemption, bearing in mind Banting's great assistance to smallholders in the county. However, Ward Davey (National Service Representative) argued that, being such a young man himself, Banting ought to allow his son to go into the Army. Mr Crawford said that tractor driving was a young man's job, and an old man could not be trained to do it. By a majority it was decided that Banting junior should be called up on 29 June. Mr Banting senior protested that he would sell his tractor (*WO* 1 June 1918). It is not clear whether Dickins or Banting actually enlisted.

80. Oliver Phillips, *Watford in the 20th Century, Volume 1,* Watford Observer, June 2011, p.78

## Gloom

Early enthusiasm for the war had disappeared by the beginning of 1917 after the appalling casualties of the year before and continuing stalemate on the Western Front. Soldiers in the trenches suffered from the coldest winter for years and conditions at home were worsening. On the Eastern Front huge numbers deserted from the Russian army and the Tsar was forced to abdicate. Although the Provisional Government launched a new offensive in the summer it failed dismally and Russia was effectively out of the war. But not all the news was bleak. The USA joined the Allies on 2 April 1917 and American troops began arriving on the Western Front in June.

The *Observer* tried to maintain morale by promoting good news and local heroes. Two promotions for Croxley men were noted (*WO* 13 January 1917): Lieutenant Frank Barton-Smith to Captain in the Loyal North Lancs Regiment; and Horace E Holloway, eldest son of Mr and Mrs Frank Holloway of Windmill House, Yorkshire and Lancashire Regiment, previously Highland Light Infantry, to 2nd Lieutenant in the King's Royal Rifle Corps.

After disaster at Kut the year before, the British offensive against the Turks in Mesopotamia regained momentum and took Baghdad in March 1917. The *Observer* pointed out that the 'Victor of Baghdad', General Maude, was a Watford resident (living in Mardale, Stratford Road for three years).[81]

Christopher Cox, from Kings Langley, gained the first Victoria Cross during the war for a resident of West Herts in May 1917:

> Private Christopher Augustus Cox No. 13908, Bedford Regiment.[82] For most conspicuous bravery and continuous devotion to duty when acting as a stretcher bearer. During the attack of his battalion the front wave was checked by the severity of enemy artillery and machine gun fire and the whole line had to take cover in shell holes to avoid annihilation. Private Cox, utterly regardless of personal safety, went out over fire swept ground and single handedly rescued four men. Having collected the wounded of his own battalion, he then assisted to bring in the wounded of the adjoining battalion. On the two subsequent days he carried out similar rescue work with the same disregard to his own personal safety. He has on all occasions displayed the same high example of unselfishness and valour.

The *Observer* continued to report on the Croxley unit of the Volunteer Training Corps under Lieutenant Raggett. The Volunteers played a games tournament with the wounded soldiers at the Croxley Hospital in February and presented Mr Barton-Smith with a framed photograph of the company (*WO* 10 February 1917).

---

81. *WO* 17 March 1917. T R Moreman, 'Maude, Sir (Frederick) Stanley (1864–1917)', *Oxford Dictionary of National Biography*, Oxford University Press, 2004; online edn, Oct 2008 [http://www.oxforddnb.com/view/article/34945, accessed 7 June 2013]
82. VC citation from the London Gazette, 11 May 1917.

# APRIL and MAY 1917 - ALLIED OFFENSIVE IN MACEDONIA

The War started in the Balkans, and in 1915 the Austrians, Germans and Bulgarians invaded Serbia. Rather than surrender, the remnants of the Serb army undertook a punishing retreat over the Albanian mountains in the winter snow. With French help the survivors managed to gain the comparative safety of Salonika in northern Greece. They were joined by French and British troops, in spite of official Greek neutrality. The Bulgarians dug in along the mountains to the north. As part of an Allied offensive, British forces attacked the Bulgarian defences on 24 April 1917 at the first battle of Doiran. The assault continued until 21 May but failed with some 5,000 British casualties. It was not until September 1918 that the Allies achieved a breakthrough in Macedonia and forced the Bulgarians to surrender.

**15 April. Private David Southam** died at sea. He was amongst the 277 who drowned when the troopship Arcadian was sunk by a U boat en route from Salonika to Alexandria in the Southern Aegean (see Neil Wheeler, *The First World War Memorials and Soldiers of Croxley Green,* and forum.gallipoli-association.org). Southam is remembered on the Mikra memorial in Salonika, Greece. He was a Private in the Army Service Corps, 904th Mechanical Transport Company. His parents, David and Elizabeth Southam, lived at 25 Dickinson Square and he would have been about 36 when he died. His parents had 12 children and in 1911 his father was a Dickinson's pensioner. David was a paper cutter at Croxley Mill. He was born at Loudwater on 17 January 1896 and baptised at All Saints' church in June.

**20 May. Private James Gatehouse Brickell** died. He is buried at Karasouli Military Cemetery, near Polikastro, Greece, which was used by casualty clearing stations for the Doiran front. Private Brickell served in the 9th Battalion, King's Own Royal Lancaster Regiment (65th Brigade, 22nd Division). James was 35 and the son of Elijah and Anna Brickell of Shaftesbury, Dorset. His widow, Annie M Brickell (nee Sears), lived at 239 New Road with Alfred and Mary Darvill. James and Annie had been married just two years.

Later in the year, the newspaper highlighted the long volunteer record of one resident from Chandlers Cross, Thomas Clode of the Clarendon Arms. At the age of 83 he claimed to be the oldest volunteer living. On 1 November 1860, he joined the 10th Tower Hamlets Rifle Volunteers, and still held his membership card. The 10th Tower Hamlets had never been disbanded so he was still considered a volunteer. Mr. Clode was well known in the neighbourhood for his amusing stories, including reminiscences of the London police of his boyhood days. He was something of a local institution and proudly wore his long service medal, publicly presented to him at the Mission Room, Chandlers Cross, by the Rev E Wells, then vicar of Croxley Green (*WO* 14 July 1917).

*Croxley Green Church Lads' Brigade about 1915 with Rev E Wells (centre left) as chaplain.*

The *Observer* also described the distinguished military and fire service record of another local resident, L W Lovett, Deputy Chief Fire Officer of Dickinson's Fire Brigade (*WO* 5 May 1917). Lewis Lovett lived at 41 Dickinson Square. He joined the 3rd City of London Volunteers in 1874 before enlisting in 1877 in the King's Dragoon Guards. He served with his regiment in South Africa, where their first duty was to bury the unfortunate men of the 24th Regiment who lost their lives at the battle of Isandlwana. He served throughout the Zulu War until after the capture of King Cetywayo, on 27 August 1879. In December 1880, Lovett was promoted sergeant. The Regiment proceeded to India where he served until 1886 including on the North West Frontier. Soon after his return home, he obtained employment with his old employers, Dickinson's, joining their private fire brigade on 25 April 1887 at Nash Mills. He was transferred to Croxley Mills in December 1894 to organise a section of the Brigade there. His combined Military and Fire Brigade service amounted to 43 years. He had attended every call to a fire since joining the Brigade.

The Church Lads' Brigade continued under the leadership of Captain Jearrad and Sergeant-Instructor Denton. In February they were inspected by Colonel Montague Jones of the Hertfordshire Regiment (*WO* 10 February 1917). In June their chaplain, the vicar of Rickmansworth, Rev F Halsey, admitted 24 new members to the Croxley and Rickmansworth Brigade at a service in St. Mary's (*WO* 23 June 1917). In September, the *Observer* recorded that the unit had formalised its paramilitary status, becoming enrolled as a cadet corps attached to the King's Royal Rifles (*WO* 15 September 1917). An entertainment took place in the Ebury Hall to raise funds for uniforms and equipment. Brigade membership was about 70 lads.

## VAD Hospital at the Dickinson Institute

The hospital depended on local volunteers to assist the regular staff in looking after the wounded servicemen. Edgar Toms' Aunt, Edie Jackson was one of the volunteers. On 22 August 1916, Edgar's mother wrote to explain, 'Auntie Edie goes to the Institute to get the soldiers' supper and wash up on Thursday evenings. She says it is a lot for one to do so I have promised to help her tonight'. On 15 April 1917, Edie wrote to Edgar, 'I still go to the Institute every Tuesday evening to get the wounded soldiers' supper. They have 36 there now, but they are altering the science room so they can have more beds, about 50 to 60 I believe altogether, so it means a little work preparing meals'.

The extra 20 beds were opened at the end of May 1917 to bring the capacity up to 50 (*WO* 2 June 1917). This made Croxley Green one of the largest VAD hospitals in the county.[83] On 31 March the *Observer* reported that the hospital had already cared for 260 wounded patients. The hospital received an important visitor on 27 August. General Mackenzie CB, General Officer Commanding 61st Division, came to present the Distinguished Conduct Medal to Sergeant H Bagenal, Royal Army Medical Corps. The sergeant had gained the award for conspicuous gallantry on the field of battle at Bernafay Wood during the Somme offensive in July 1916. He had been in charge of stretcher bearers for 48 hours under shell fire.

The hospital quarter-master, Miss Barton-Smith, kept autograph books for the patients to write in. Three of them have survived, now in the Three Rivers Museum Trust collection, and they make a splendid record. Naturally, the soldiers wanted to be complimentary about the care they had received but their gratitude to the nurses and staff has a ring of truth. For most patients, staying at the hospital was a peaceful interlude in a stressful time and they found the camaraderie rewarding.

Some were just pleased to be there. 'Tres bon Angleterre' wrote Rifleman E Roberts, Rifle Brigade, who was wounded through the neck on 28 August 1916. Another soldier contributed:

> Breathes there the man with soul so dead,
> Who never himself hath said
> This is my own, my native land
> "Blighty"
> A free trip.

---

83. The largest was Royston with 52 beds. Beryl Carrington, *Care in Crisis: Hertfordshire British Red Cross 1907-1994,* Baron Birch 1995.

# APRIL 1917 - BRITISH OFFENSIVE AT ARRAS

The Allies decided on a further offensive on the Western Front in the spring of 1917. The British, under overall French command, were to attack at Arras before the French sought to overwhelm German positions further south on the Chemin des Dames ridge between Soissons and Rheims. The British assault commenced on 6 April and gained some initial success, notably the capture by Canadian forces of Vimy Ridge (9 to 12 April). However, the British soon stalled and the French attack suffered the same fate. The Allies took heavy casualties. The French failure prompted mutiny amongst French troops and led to Petain taking over military leadership.

Four, possibly five, Croxley men died in the Arras offensive.

---

**6 April. Lance Corporal Arthur William Jefford** died. He is buried in Barlin communal cemetery extension south of Bethune. The cemetery extension was used for burials by the 6th Casualty Clearing Station which was located in the town. Lance Corporal Jefford served in A Company, 73rd Battalion Canadian Infantry and in the Canadian Field Ambulance. He was born on 2 August 1893 in St Albans and was 23 when he died. In 1911 he lived with his parents, Ernest William and Ellen Jefford, in Croxley Hall Farm Cottages. The family were farm labourers who seem to have moved around from farm to farm in the Watford and St. Albans area. Arthur emigrated to Canada. When he enlisted on 6 February 1916 he was living at 25 Gore St., Sault Ste Marie, Ontario and he set sail for Europe from Halifax on SS Metagama on 8 August 1916. Ernest and Ellen were still at Croxley Hall in 1918 but subsequently moved to Berkhamsted.

**11 April. Lance Corporal Ernest Mead** died of wounds. He is buried in Aubigny communal cemetery extension, north west of Arras. The cemetery was used by a number of casualty clearing stations in the area. Lance Corporal Mead served in the 1st/6th Battalion, Seaforth Highlanders and was 23 when he died. He was born in Croxley on 15 September 1893, the second son of George and Fanny Mead of 179 New Road. George and Fanny had six children. Like his father, Ernest was a labourer at Croxley Mills.

 **28 April. Private Benjamin Bastin** died. He is remembered on the Arras memorial. Private Bastin served in the 17th Battalion (Duke of Cambridge's Own) Middlesex Regiment and was 28 when he died. His parents, John and Jane Bastin, lived at Chenies and, after the war, his widow, Harriet Bastin lived in Bristol. In 1911, Benjamin worked as a domestic gardener at the Gardens, Loudwater. In 1901 he was living with his parents, two brothers and two sisters at 4 Chesham Road, Chenies.

**3 May. Lance Corporal Frederick John Sansom** died. He is remembered on the Arras memorial. Lance Corporal Sansom served in the 4th Battalion, Royal Fusiliers (City of London Regiment). Frederick was the eldest child of Harry and Lily Sansom of Cassiobridge. He helped his father run their watercress business. Both he and his father were born in Redbourn. The family seem to have moved to the Rickmansworth area about 1900. His mother (nee Luckett) came from Abbots Langley. Frederick would have been about 20 when he died.

*Stretcher bearers deal with casualties.*

**14 May. Gunner Herbert Bertram Mason** died of wounds at Richmond and is buried in Chorleywood Road Cemetery, Rickmansworth. Gunner Mason served in 140th Siege Battery, Royal Garrison Artillery. The 140th Battery went to France in August 1916 and Herbert may have been another casualty of the Arras offensive. He was 25 when he died and the husband of Annie Mason, 14 Scots Hill. No 1911 census record for him in the locality has been found but, according to Neil Wheeler (*The First World War Memorials and Soldiers of Croxley Green*, 1995) he was born in Amersham. Herbert married Annie (nee Gilbey) in the last quarter of 1911. Annie was 28 in 1911, and a factory paper sorter living with her parents at 4 Cherry Tree Cottages, Croxley Green. The *Observer* of 23 June 1917 refers to him as a resident of Croxley Green.

*Above: convalescing servicemen outside the Dickinson Institute in 1918.*

*Below: a patient being tended in the sick bay.*

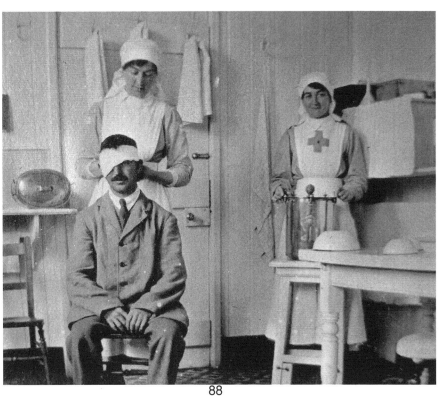

*The hospital kitchen at the Dickinson Institute*

Some compared favourably their prized digs in Croxley with 'that dead hole Napsbury' as one put it (i.e. the Middlesex War Hospital). The Croxley hospital was 'home from home' for many of them and it was a happy place. They flattered the nurses and volunteers, and poked fun mildly at the food and strictness of the hospital regime. Sergeant W Sleight of the Royal Army Medical Corps wrote in 1916 about the life-saving work of the Red Cross 'that raises the fallen'. In 1918, Driver MacGregor of the Royal Field Artillery called them 'the world's greatest power'.

Some of the soldiers used their page in the book to recall the experiences at the front to which they would soon return. On 20 November 1916, Rifleman H Lauterback of 16 Rifle Brigade quoted a parody of a popular song, well known amongst soldiers at the time:

> Sing me to sleep where the bullets fall,
> Let me forget the world and all,
> Damp is my dugout,
> Cold are my feet,
> And there's nothing but bully and biscuits to eat.

The song goes on about the corpses in front of the sandbags, the German snipers, the worms and the rats. Private W Crighton of the 7th Black Watch anticipated in a rhyme, on 22 February 1917, that he would leave for the front and be gassed but

*Soldiers in the ward upstairs at the Dickinson Institute*

Croxley would stay with him as a happy memory. Private W B Nickson of the Manchester Regiment summed it up, 'Once bit, twice shy'. Drummer W W Hilton of the 1st Royal Irish Rifles was more phlegmatic. 'Joined up in 1904, went to India 1907. Come home in 1914. Went to France 1914 and got wounded in same year, out to France same year, home 1915, out 1916 home same year. Hoping to see the end.'

**Croxley Green's Australians**

A number of the patients at the Croxley Green hospital were Australian soldiers. At Christmas 1917, 51 patients signed the book of whom 17 were Australians.

Corporal Will G Lane, No 2 Company, Australian Miners, left the following romantic verse in 1916:

> Remember me, when this you see
> Tho' many miles apart
> Others may have my company
> But you have got my heart
> Now to you my heart is given
> So please give yours to me
> Then I will lock them both together
> And throw away the key.

Unfortunately, Corporal Lane's stay at Croxley Green did not cure him. He came from the mining city of Broken Hill, New South Wales, and joined up in October 1915 at the age of 38. He was sent to the Western Front as a specialist miner, where he arrived in May 1916. But he only lasted a few weeks in the trenches before contracting what the medical records show as 'chronic nephritis' or inflammation of the kidneys. The

90

medical report points out that conditions in the trenches at the time were wet and foul. A medical board found him unfit for further service and he was repatriated to his wife and family in April 1917. Sadly he died on 4 May 1918 and is buried in Adelaide.

Another Australian was impressed by the hospital. Private Francis Marek, 25th Battalion Australian Imperial Force, wrote a verse comparing Croxley to heaven. He must have been sincere because, on 12 April 1917, he was married at All Saints' church to a local girl, Esther Sanders of 38 Dickinson Square. Francis was taken sick with septicaemia in June 1916 and, after recovering at Croxley, he was posted to a training battalion in Wiltshire. However, on 14 April 1918 he was severely wounded in the chest by shell fragments and was taken to the Australian hospital at Harefield for an operation. Thankfully this must have been successful because he returned to Australia in June 1918, presumably with his new wife, and was discharged from the army the following October.

A third Australian, Private Thomas Walter Jarvie, 19th Battalion Australian Imperial Force, made an unusual contribution to the autograph book in February 1917. He quoted from the Elizabethan poet and dramatist Samuel Daniel (1562-1619). Jarvie was keen to convey that it is hardship which brings out the best in people:

> and we come to know
> best what men are in their worst jeopardies;
> for lo, how many have we seen to grow
> to high renown, from lowest miseries,

Thomas Jarvie was a somewhat unusual recruit when he enlisted in New South Wales in 1915. He was a 28 year old school teacher. After working in the military stores in Alexandria for 6 months he eventually got to the Western Front in 1916. But there he found the fatigues physically impossible and, after four months in the trenches, he was hospitalised with 'trench feet' in December 1916. How he passed the enlistment medical is hard to understand. He was born with club feet which were straightened but the operation left him with thin, underdeveloped legs. The doctors concluded that he was unfitted for the infantry. Consequently he was transferred to administrative work and made good progress. By July 1918 he was promoted to Sergeant and working in London. He married a local girl in June 1920 and was finally discharged, at the rank of Warrant Officer, in July 1921, to live in Brixton Hill, London.

## Congratulations to a Croxley Green Nurse

A local girl, May Morriss, was one woman to claim some prominence in the *Observer's* pages, thanks to her skill as a nurse. Her mother was a widow, Mrs A Morriss, of Croxley Green. May had been appointed Night Sister at the Royal Victoria Hospital, Folkestone, Kent. She was trained at the General Military Hospital, Edmonton, where she won the gold medal for practical nursing. According to the *Observer's* informant, she was a great favourite with both the staff and the patients at Edmonton and they were sorry to see her go. Miss Morriss said that she would like to be nursing in France, as far up the line as they would allow. She would far rather be in the thick of it out there, where she would feel of some real use to the country. However, there was important work to be done at home too and, according to the *Observer,* she was probably one of the youngest nurses in the country to become a Night Sister (*WO* 4 August 1917).

## All Saints' War Shrine Unveiled

Rev Charles H Blois-Bisshopp became the new vicar of Croxley Green on 3 March 1917, after being curate in Watford for five years. One of his early concerns was the commemoration of those serving in the armed forces. He proposed to the Easter Vestry meeting that a war shrine should be erected outside the church with the names of all those from the village who served in the armed forces. The Vestry meeting agreed and All Saints' sought funds by a special subscription.

*Rev Charles Blois-Bisshopp*

The village war shrine was dedicated and unveiled on Sunday 29 July 1917. The *Observer* reported that the memorial to the 320 brave men of Croxley who had enlisted had been placed in the extreme south-western corner of the churchyard. Outside, opposite it, hundreds of people stood in the pouring rain, while the church building was filled to capacity. After singing the hymn, 'O God our help in ages past', the choir, the vicar, the churchwardens (Mr C Barton-Smith and Mr E C Trench), the Church Lads' Brigade, and the congregation processed from the church into the churchyard under the watchful eyes of Special Constables. In the rain, the vicar unveiled the shrine, while the band of the Church Lads' Brigade sounded the salute, and everyone sang the three verses of the National Anthem. Prevented by the weather from speaking outside, the vicar led the congregation back into the church where he reminded them that they had come together to honour the living and the dead. Each of the 320 names on the shrine represented a sacrifice of home comforts, of family and friends. Some of the names represented the great sacrifice: the giving up of life itself. Blois-Bisshopp said that the shrine was a call to remembrance and to prayer: for the living that they might be preserved, for the dead that they might have rest. He added that the war was not only about men, but also women, and the mothers of Croxley had bravely done their part by sending their sons. He felt sure that the great cost would not be in vain and, when Great Britain had passed through the cloud into the sunshine again, it would be a better purer country, with higher ideals of the Fatherhood of God and the brotherhood of man.....

The *Observer* described the shrine as Jacobean in style, and made of wainscot oak, with the inscription at the top, 'your prayers are asked for those who have gone forth from this parish to serve their King and country, whether by land, by sea or by air'. The names of 320 parishioners known to be serving or to have served were painted below. Those in the Navy are in blue, and those in the Army in red. The shrine was designed by Mr W E Edwards of Croxley Green, and made by John Thompson and

*29 July 1917. Unveiling All Saints' shrine.*
*Summer frocks, hats and umbrellas. Note the mourning family right foreground.*

Sons of Peterborough.[84] The minutes of All Saints' Church Council on 18 October 1917 record that £55 was raised for the shrine, which cost £40.

## Croxley Mills

The *Observer* reported two fatalities at Croxley Mills during 1917. In January, Harry Humphreys was run over by some trucks in the mill siding and killed (*WO* 13 January 1917). Then on 28 November John Taylor (45) of Chester Rd Watford was killed after a truck fell on top of him when some staging broke (*WO* 8 December 1917).

The mill experienced shortages in 1917 when the government cut imports of papermaking materials to half the quantity imported in 1916. As a result the company had to shut down one machine. Then in May 1917 the mill became a 'Controlled Establishment' under the Ministry of Munitions. Consequently about 80 per cent of output was supplied to the government or those on the government's priority list. Dickinson's as a whole used their card department at Apsley to manufacture boards for food containers, for packing munitions and for other government purposes. This left little paper for ordinary consumers and the company had to resort to careful rationing to keep its customers supplied at all. This was clearly a difficult time for the

84. John Thompson and Sons was founded in the late 1810s or early 1820s and specialised in ecclesiastical restoration, church furniture and institutional buildings. The firm closed in 1938. See www.nationalarchives.gov.uk/nra.onlinelists/GB0281%20JT.pdf (accessed 14 June 2013).

management. Nonetheless, they succeeded in earning good profits during the war period. In 1915, 1916 and 1917 shareholders benefited from dividends at 10 per cent and bonuses of from 2 to 5 per cent.[85]

## Nigel Newall is killed

*Second Lieutenant Nigel Newall*

Nigel Newall was the youngest of the Newalls' three sons and the second to be killed in action. The third son, Keith, served in the Navy. Nigel volunteered immediately war was declared, became a member of the Honourable Artillery Company, and went out to France on 17 September 1914. He served all that winter in Flanders and came home on 5 May to take a commission as Second Lieutenant in the Welsh Guards. Nigel returned to join that regiment at the Front on 5 November 1915. He was shot through both legs on 20 January 1916, invalided home, and returned to 1st Battalion Welsh Guards on 26 June 1917, just in time to take part in the Third Battle of Ypres (Passchendaele). He was killed on 12 October 1917, just 21 years old. By October, the conditions the troops had to contend with were appalling. Wet weather had turned the battlefield into a morass of deep mud and pools of stagnant water with corpses everywhere. According to the memorial in All Saints' church, Nigel was buried on the battlefield close to Houthulst Forest, near Louvois Farm. However, after the war had ended, his grave was never found and he is now remembered on Tyne Cot memorial to the missing alongside almost 35,000 others who lost their lives in the battles of the Ypres salient.

A close friend of Nigel's, Percy Baltye, was with him when he died and wrote to his mother offering his deepest sympathy:

> Dear Mrs Newall,
> I cannot tell you how sorry I am to have to tell you that Nigel was killed instantaneously on Friday morning at 3 minutes past 6.
>
> All my officers had been wounded, and he was sent to help me as I was in a rather bad unpleasant place with no officers. The Germans were being heavily shelled and he and I were watching from our shell hole to see if the Germans were going to retire, and we would then have shot them and followed them, and as Nigel got up to shoot at some of the

85. Joan Evans, *The Endless Web*, p. 184

enemy he was hit by a bullet in the middle of his forehead. He fell back stone dead in my arms. I cannot tell you how dreadfully sorry I am for you. He was such a splendid person and was simply worshipped by his men and loved by all of us, he will be most terribly missed.

It was a great blow to both of us that he did not come to my company, but all the same we managed to see a lot of each other. I think he looked on me as his best friend, as we were the only men of the old lot left out here. It is so terribly sad, I cannot get over it. We were so pleased to be together those few hours, and he behaved so well, especially as I was dead tired, and he worked very hard for me to try and give me a rest and I feel his death very deeply indeed.

The post is just going, so I must hurry up with what I have left to tell you. He was buried here yesterday morning a hundred yards from where he fell. After he was killed I went through his pockets to send you back anything. As I was doing so a shell burst and knocked me and my orderly over and buried us, so I fear that some of the few personal private effects that he had with him are lost. I know there was a small pig that he loved, but it was buried, also his watch. The orderly was taken straight to hospital, I shall go to see him today and find if he saved anything. The only things I have are his identity disc and his cigarette case, which if you will allow me to, I am very anxious to keep till the end of the war, and if I get killed I will see it is returned to you. I fear this letter is very disjointed, but I've only just come out of the line. We have had the hardest time I have ever had and for once I feel rather shaken and most terribly sad. With my love and my very deepest sympathies,
Yours very sincerely,
Percy Baltye

P S I particularly want a photograph of Nigel if you would be kind enough to send me one. I will write again tomorrow. Just before he was killed, we were talking about home and other things, and his last words to me about one minute before he was killed were, 'Thank God, Percy, we are out here, and not winning the war in England'.[86]

The Newalls were the second Croxley family, after the Goodmans, to lose two sons in the conflict. It affected them deeply and William Newall applied to All Saints' for permission to erect a memorial to Leslie and Nigel.[87] The church agreed and the plaque is one of the few personal memorials inside All Saints'.

Nigel Newall's comment about those 'winning the war' in England was, perhaps, appropriate for some not too far from his home of Redheath. The *Observer* reported a meeting of the West Herts War Aims Committee which included representatives of the three political parties (*WO* 27 October 1917). They passed enthusiastically a

86. Reproduced with permission from Patrick Moore, '*A History of Redheath and York House School*', Triflower Press 2010 p.6.
87. Minutes of a Special Vestry Meeting, 6 December 1917, All Saints' church.

resolution expressing inflexible determination to carry on the war until the aims of the Allies were fully achieved. And they did this when it must have been obvious that the Eastern Front was crumbling and Russia was effectively out of the war. The Bolshevik revolution took place on 26 October. The only bright spot was the progress made against the Turks. British forces under Allenby entered Jerusalem on 9 December.

*Stretcher bearers in Flanders' mud*

# PASSCHENDAELE, THE THIRD BATTLE OF YPRES, JULY TO NOVEMBER 1917

After modest success further south at Messines Ridge in June 1917, the British launched a major offensive at Ypres on 31 July 1917. The Germans were well prepared and the British attacks finally petered out in the Flanders mud at the beginning of November. The offensive had pushed the British lines forward about 4 miles onto the Passchendaele ridge but at the cost of over 310,000 Allied casualties. The Hertfordshire Regiment was involved at St Julien in August, where they were overwhelmed with heavy losses, including Colonel Page and many other officers killed. Five men from Croxley perished in the offensive.

# CROXLEY MEN WHO DIED AT PASSCHENDAELE JULY TO NOVEMBER 1917

All five are remembered on the Tyne Cot memorial to the missing.

**Sergeant Harry Chapman** died on 21 September aged 26. He was one of the Church Lads who joined the 16th KRRC at the outset and was killed while serving in A Company, 18th Battalion, King's Royal Rifle Corps. Harry was born in Croxley on 5 September 1890. His parents, John and Mary Chapman, lived at 331 New Road. Like his father and brother, Harry worked for Croxley Mills. In 1911 he was employed as a clerk. He had four siblings.

**Lance Corporal John Newman** died on 4 October. He served in 2nd Battalion, Seaforth Highlanders (Ross-shire Buffs), and previously in the Bedfordshire Regiment. John was 21 when he died. His parents were Alfred and Hannah Newman and the family lived in Tudor Cottage on the Green. In 1911 Alfred was a coachman and John worked for a building firm as an apprentice carpenter and joiner. The *Observer* of 10 November reported that a few weeks before his death he had been offered a commission, and was expected home. The chaplain wrote to John's sister, 'Your brother was in charge of a Lewis gun team on 4 October when he was hit in the head by a sniper and killed instantaneously. The Colonel, officers and men, join in sending deepest sympathy at the loss of your gallant brother. He was greatly liked by his comrades and was regarded as an efficient soldier. He is much missed in his platoon'.

**Second Lieutenant Nigel Newall** died on 12 October, aged 22, 1st Battalion Welsh Guards. (See main text.)

**Private Herbert James Jeffery** died on 25 October. He served in the 1st Battalion Bedfordshire Regiment. Herbert was 17 in 1911, so he would have been about 23 when he died. He was born in Mill Hill, Middlesex. Herbert's parents were Charles and Laura Jeffery. Charles was a farm bailiff working at Maxal Farm, North Cray, Chislehurst, Kent in 1901. In 1911 Charles referred to himself as a disengaged farm bailiff and the family had moved to 38 Talbot Road in Rickmansworth. Herbert was working as a builder's clerk. He lived at 132 New Road with his wife Cissie. They had a son Richard Walter Jeffery who was baptised at All Saints' on 29 November 1916 (Neil Wheeler).

**Gunner Samuel William Newberry** died on 3 November. He served in D Battery, 46th Brigade, Field Artillery. Samuel was the son of Matthew and Jane Newberry of the Duke of York public house, Croxley Green. They put an advert in the *Observer* of 24 November 1917 to thank friends for their sympathy. In 1911 the Newberry family lived at 66 Church Street, Rickmansworth. At that time, Matthew was a steam crane driver for a gravel company and Samuel, aged about 19, was a steam crane fireman.

## News from the Front

In 1917, there were notably less of the morale-boosting stories in the *Observer* compared to 1915 and reports of Croxley men, apart from those killed in action, were sparse. However, one Croxley man, Bombardier Bert Waller, Royal Garrison Artillery, was awarded the Military Medal for bravery in the field (*WO* 25 August 1917). He volunteered to connect up telephonic communications and worked for 48 hours under shell fire and gas attack until the task was finished. Among those local men who were wounded were Stanley Beament (*WO* 22 September 1917), F Adams (11 KRRC) (*WO* 24 November 1917), and Sergeant A Owen (Royal Garrison Artillery) (*WO* 1 December 1917).

## Memorial service at All Saints'

Following the practice of previous years, the new vicar of All Saints', Rev Blois-Bisshopp, led an impressive memorial service to the men of the parish who had fallen in the war, on the evening of All Soul's Day, 2 November. The service began with hymns and part of the burial service. Then amid silence the Vicar read out the names of the following 30 men of Croxley Green who had given their lives for their country: -

> Arthur Toms, John Walker, John Gardner, Leslie Newall, Cecil Wheeler, Frederick Elbourne, John Goodman, Frederick Randall, Frank Arnold, Charles Strugnell, Cecil Gravestock, Wilfred Warn, Leonard Pitkin, Walter Element, Charles Rogers, Maurice Neale, Frederick Groom, Arthur Jefford, William Goodman, Frank Hobbs, James Lyons, James Brickell, William Woollams, William Carter, Ernest Mead, Herbert Mason, David Southam, Harry Chapman, Nigel Newall and John Newman.

Then in a short address the vicar emphasised the values of service and sacrifice. The men whose names had been read out knew that war meant privation, pain, suffering, and might mean death, but they did not flinch. They had died for their faith like the martyrs of old, and had passed on to a deathless life. After the National Anthem, the 'Last Post' was sounded by ex-Sergeant Gudgin, ex-Sergeant Hawtin, and Corporal Hunt, all of the Church Lads' Brigade. The choir was directed by W Acton Gittins, organist and choirmaster (*WO* 10 November 1917).

The 30 men listed by the vicar at the service omit two, Frederick Clarke and Robert Duley, who were included by his predecessor in 1916. Clarke is listed on the shrine and war memorial but Duley is not. Others omitted are Benjamin Bastin, Frederick Sansom and Herbert Jeffery. Jeffery's death was probably too recent to be included.

## The *Observer's* Review of the Year

The editor of the *Observer* strove to sustain morale at home by lauding the record of gallantry and sacrifice from the Hertfordshire and Bedfordshire regiments and listing the many awards won by soldiers from West Herts and the county as a whole, including six Victoria Crosses. He pointed out that the Volunteers had done excellent work. All fit and efficient members of the Volunteer Regiment had been provided with rifles. Some 450 soldiers from Watford had been killed in action and the chairman of the hospital committee, Mr E Henry Lloyd of Langleybury, had appealed for the construction of a new District Hospital as a local war memorial.

In Croxley, the year ended with Christmas carols in the Girls' School and Mr H T Wilson's annual talk. The newspaper noted the usual large attendance. Neggy's subject was 'Blind Man's Buff', but his talk was a 'clever, scientific interpretation of the causes of existing customs'. According to the *Observer* many of the carols were 'quaint and uncompromising'.

The soldiers recuperating in the hospital enjoyed a full social programme at Christmas too with Charles Barton-Smith supervising. This included the usual weekly whist drive, a concert and on Christmas Day, 'an abundance of good cheer'. 51 soldiers signed the Quartermaster's (May Barton-Smith) autograph book at the Christmas dinner. 17 of them were Australians. The night sister W C S Blundell was there too as was May's sister Maud and other guests. Charles Barton-Smith signed himself as 'Chairman of the best Christmas dinner party in the world or at least none better'. In the afternoon and evening the soldiers themselves organised a social gathering, inviting their friends. Then, on Boxing Day they performed a couple of plays to full houses (*WO* 29 December 1917).

*Convalescing soldiers on the Green*

# 1918

The year began quietly on the Western Front. British forces were exhausted after Passchendaele. Judging by the *Observer*, there was not a great deal to report in Croxley Green either. All Saints' church held a missionary week; the YMCA campaigned to raise funds to equip a 'Watford and District' hut to support the troops; and the Croxley Green Ladies' Choral Class gave an excellent concert, coached by Miss Byron and Mr Veale, the local piano teacher. Two Croxley men were reported wounded, Lance-Corporal J E Hull, King's Royal Rifle Corps, and A Ford, Middlesex Regiment. Henry Richard Scobell, the only son of the late W Scobell of Dickinson Square, was gazetted a Second Lieutenant in the Royal Flying Corps.

## Conscription and Small Businesses in Croxley Green

As the demand for recruits became ever more insistent it was more and more difficult for small local businesses to keep going. The Rickmansworth Military Service Tribunal had to decide whether the work concerned was of national importance and therefore whether their staff deserved exemption.

There was one Croxley enterprise which gained full support from the tribunal: the blacksmiths in New Road run by the Gibbs family. James Gibbs of 46 New Road who worked as an agricultural smith was given an absolute exemption. So was W Chapman of Hagden Lane, Watford, who worked for Jesse Gibbs as a wheelwright and farrier. Gibbs said that Chapman repaired every kind of machinery used on a farm and the tribunal exempted him because he was in a certified occupation.

George Ide (aged 41) found himself in a similar situation. He was a motor engineer, living at 'Yeoveny' in Watford Road who managed the works for George Jones and Sons, Coachbuilders and Motor Engineers, Church Street Rickmansworth.[88] He had been working on government controlled agricultural tractors. However, the tribunal did not give him an easy ride. Ide was called before the tribunal five times and had to argue his case. Nevertheless he succeeded in getting his conditional exemption renewed throughout the war.

Like the blacksmiths, local bakers and butchers were granted absolute exemption in 1916 but this changed as the war dragged on. For example, Arthur Dorrell (39) baker, Percy Singleton foreman baker at the Co-op and Jeremiah Sanders butcher (aged 38 of 96 New Road) were granted absolute exemption in July 1916. However, Singleton (142 New Road) enlisted in 1917 and served as a Private in 12th Field Battery, Army Service Corps. Dorrell and Sanders had to apply to the tribunal again in 1918 to maintain their exemptions. Fred Harrison (aged 29 of Cherry Cottages, Scots Hill), was butcher's manager in charge of Fletcher's Rickmansworth branch

88. See *Rickmansworth Historical Society Newsletter* article on John and George Jones, issue 79 (2008).

and had been exempted too. However, this was successfully challenged by the Military Representative in January 1917. Harrison joined up a few months later and served as a Gunner in the Royal Field Artillery in Mesopotamia.

Other businesses had a protracted wrangle with the tribunal in an attempt to keep their key workers. Harold Aitken (35) of 127 New Road was a shop assistant at Messrs Beeson and Sons, Church Street, Rickmansworth.[89]    Beesons was an important local business involved in building, ironmongery, builders' supplies and small scale engineering work. They were finding it hard to keep going when several members of staff were called up. Mr Beeson argued to the tribunal in September 1917 that Aitken was the only man left in the shop and his work could not be done by a woman. But the tribunal was only prepared to grant exemption until the end of November. Beesons appealed successfully to the County Tribunal who granted a six months conditional exemption. The firm was back at the County Tribunal in April 1918 and was refused. According to the 1918 absent voters' list, Harold Aitken joined the 3rd Buffs (Royal East Kent Regiment) as a Private.

The Croxley Green Laundry found itself in a similar position. The proprietor, Mr B C Cheetham, argued that his boilerman, Percival Green (aged 29 of 262 New Road), should be exempt because he was the only man on the premises and Cheetham had advertised five times without receiving a single reply. He would have to close down if Green went into the army. The tribunal allowed six months' exemption in August 1916 provided that Green joined the special constables. In June 1917, Cheetham was back before the tribunal arguing that substitutes sent from the Labour Exchange had proved useless. The Military Representative said that Green was a priority for enlistment because he was classed A and under 31. The tribunal gave a further two months' exemption and Cheetham was instructed to do his best to find a substitute. He tried for more leniency by appealing to the County Tribunal but they confirmed the decision. The last record of this case in the *Observer* is in September 1917, when despite Cheetham's arguments about the impossibility of finding a substitute, the Tribunal decided that the exemption should only last until the end of November. Green enlisted and, in 1918, was an Air Mechanic in 118 Squadron, RAF. Finally, Cheetham himself (aged 39) was forced to apply to the tribunal in October 1918 but managed to gain exemption.

The Croxley Green Co-operative Society failed to prevent their vanman and bakery assistant, G Mead (24), being called up early in 1917. However, they were more successful with respect to the manager, George Kingham (aged 38 of Yorke Road). He was granted conditional exemption in May and December 1917. Kingham's case was examined again in October 1918 and by then he held a protection certificate, obtained by the Co-operative Society.

In contrast, Wallis' builders and decorators was not so successful. Charles Herbert Wallis (24) of 3 New Road argued that his father could not run the business alone if he was called up. But the tribunal was having none of it and both he and Henry Robert Revell, who worked for the Wallis family, were required to enlist in 1916. In 1918,

89. See *Rickmansworth Historical Society Newsletter* article on Beesons, issue 53 (June 2001).

Wallis was an Air Mechanic in the RAF but Revell was living at home in Copthorne Cottages.

Henry Sharman was 35 when he first appeared before the tribunal in April 1917. He was a hairdresser and lived at 226 New Road. Although hairdressing could hardly be described as a vital contribution to the war effort, Sharman managed to remain exempt, provided he joined the special constables, until the end of the war. The reason appears to be his lack of medical fitness.

Overall, small businesses suffered badly from the loss of staff, especially those dependent on one or two men, and it usually was men in those days. Employers were reluctant even to consider taking on women instead. Recruiting so many able-bodied men from Croxley Green placed everyone's lives under stress. Women had to expand their roles, families had to try to make ends meet and those left with the responsibility of running businesses had to cope with increasing burdens. Nonetheless, most businesses, even Wallis' builders and the Croxley Green Laundry, managed to survive these difficult times.

### The VAD Hospital at the Dickinson Institute

The VAD Hospital at the Dickinson Institute received official recognition when its commandant, Mrs Florence Kennedy, was one of a number of Red Cross staff commended to the Secretary of State for rendering valuable service in the administration of hospitals (*WO* 9 February 1918). The hospital itself was closed for cleaning at the beginning of February and the 49 patients were sent back to the County of Middlesex War Hospital at Napsbury. The Croxley hospital reopened at the end of March (*WO* 6 April 1918).

*Patients leave for Napsbury.*

*Croxley Green VAD Hospital staff, patients and Bruce the mascot, 1918*

*The hospital management. From left to right: Sister Nicholas, Commandant Florence Kennedy, Quartermaster May Barton-Smith, Treasurer Charles Barton-Smith*

Patients at the hospital were encouraged to entertain themselves. There was a band, of sorts, and they put on musical evenings and plays. In February 1917 a visiting minister, Rev P Stanley, had embroidered a popular song, 'Down Zummerzett Way', by adding a verse in honour of the hospital, '....If you want to have a good old time why Croxley's the place I say. You play your billiards, smoke your fag, and sing your songs to a good old rag...'.

*The hospital 'band' on the Green and billiards in the Institute (below).*

*Left, scrubbing day at the hospital*

*Below, the sick bay*

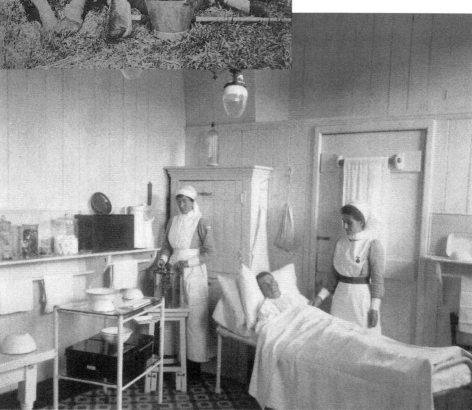

Above - The garden fete given for hospital patients by Mr and Mrs Hyman at Harewood Place, Chorleywood Road on Saturday 6 July 1918. The Barton-Smith family in evidence; May front centre, Frank standing centre and Charles seated centre left.

Left - the 'kitchen team'.

*Recreation for recuperating soldiers at the Dickinson Institute: (above) the cast of 'The Wayward Son' including the author, Private Hyams, with beard.*

Then on 3 December 1917 the hospital players put on a performance of 'The Wayward Son', written by Private Maurice Hyams, 36th Battalion Australian Imperial Force. Hyams was also one of the stars. He was recovering from a wound in his shoulder suffered in October in Belgium.

## Electoral Reform

On the broader national stage, the local MP, Arnold Ward, demonstrated the changing face of the country when he announced that he would retire as Conservative and Unionist candidate (*WO* 23 February 1918). Ward's strong support for the Ulster rebels, his patriotism and his early enlistment with the Hertfordshire Yeomanry have already been noted. He had taken part in the Middle East campaign. Ward was strongly opposed to granting voting rights to women and he returned temporarily to his parliamentary duties in April 1917 to organise the opposition to women's suffrage in the Electoral Reform bill. He failed, and large numbers of women were enfranchised in the Representation of the People Act passed in February 1918. The *Observer* recorded Ward's comment, which is a bit hard to credit, that now the enfranchisement of women was an accomplished fact, there was no other thought in his mind but to help women voters. Perhaps he felt that the best way to help them was to give way to another candidate.

## Croxley Green Girls' School

The war affected the lives of schoolchildren, not least because fathers and brothers were fighting in the forces.[90]  In addition, the school log book reveals subtle ways in which the children were involved.  The school encouraged its pupils to broaden their interests beyond the Empire to include the Allies.  On 18 November 1915 the girls spent 5s 2d to purchase Russian flags. The girls were involved in knitting socks for soldiers during the cold winter of 1917.[91]  They also proved adept at raising money for war-related causes.  In November 1916 they put on a concert in aid of the Kitchener Memorial Fund, which raised 11s 11d.[92]  During the Christmas holidays at the end of 1916 they collected £1 1s 10d for the relief of Belgian children.  On Empire Day they raised money for the Overseas Club (9s in 1917 and 11s 4½d in 1918) and in June 1918 they raised 4s 4½d for blind soldiers.  Moreover, the school encouraged pupils to use their savings to support the war.  In September 1916 Miss Stanford mentioned that 12 girls had started War Savings Cards and 30 belonged to the Penny Bank.

The school also collaborated with Croxley Mills.  In May 1918 the management provided £1 to be distributed to the children bringing the most waste paper.  In May, Maisie Davis received 5s and Annie Furr 1s and, in June, Irene Pitkin received 4s and Gwen Oliver 2s. Miss Stanford noted, 'We pay the money in stamps on a War Savings Certificate'.  She was always on the lookout for money to supplement the school's small budget and so she was glad to note in the log book for May 1918, 'Waste paper funds were used to contribute to the cost (£3 12s 2d) of a netball set and a book, 'The Epic' by H A Guerber costing 12s 6d'.[93]

Miss Stanford noted one unusual by-product of the war on 8 March 1918:
> On Tuesday March 5th I left school in the afternoon to play at the Funeral Service for Mr Clode.  My class remained in charge of the two prefects. Wednesday morning these girls asked if a court martial might be held on four girls who had been somewhat troublesome during my absence.  Some weeks back the class tried one girl and certainly she has made a greater effort since – so I gave permission for the so-called court martial.

But the war did not dominate everything.  On 9 July 1918 the head mistress noted, 'The first class girls brought their tea to school this afternoon and at 3.30 we set out for the Strawberry fields about 3 miles away.[94]  On the way back there was a heavy storm so we sheltered in Chandlers Cross Church – the girls singing their favourite hymns.' Miss Stanford also celebrated the achievements of some of the girls.  Three

---

90.  This section is drawn from the log book of Croxley Green National School 1916 to 1918
91.  Letter from Lizzie Toms to Edgar Toms, 8 February 1917.
92.  The Lord Kitchener National Memorial Fund began in June 1916 to raise funds for the relief of disabled officers and men.  Kitchener died on 5 June 1916 when the ship on which he was sailing hit a mine and sank (see lknmf.com accessed 28 January 2014).
93.  Helene Guerber wrote many books dealing with ancient myths and legends at around this period. *The Epic* summarises many of them for the benefit of 'young students or the busy general reader' see www.gutenberg.org
94.  Strawberry Fields was a clearing in Whippendell Woods.

girls, Kitty Coleman, Frances Haviland and Phoebe Lipscombe, were highly commended for an essay on 'a personality of the war' in the July number of 'Little Folks' and Dora Jenner, Olive Young, Olive Payne, Kitty Coleman and Annie Partington were highly commended for a pen and ink sketch illustrating a story.[95]

Each summer the girls joined the boys in school sports. Miss Stanford noted with pride on 30 July 1918 that the girls had won the tug of war between girls and boys. They repeated the feat in 1919.

---

# 1918 - THE GERMAN SPRING OFFENSIVE

On the Western Front things were about to change for the worse. Russia surrendered to Germany on 3 March, thus making possible a single-minded German focus on Britain and France. Faced with shortages of men and supplies at home and threatened by America abroad, the German leadership decided to gamble on a major offensive to defeat the British before the Americans could arrive in strength.

The **German Spring Offensive** began on 21 March with an assault across the Somme battlefields which they had fought over in 1916. They shattered the British Fifth Army and drove the British back 40 miles with 290,000 casualties including many taken prisoner. But the defenders held firm to the east of Amiens and the attack ran out of steam on 4 April. The Allies appointed Foch as overall commander to coordinate their resistance. A second phase of the German offensive was launched in Flanders on 9 April but that too was halted by the end of the month. On 27 May the Germans attacked again, this time to the south across the Chemin des Dames ridge between Soissons and Rheims. The Allies halted them at the River Marne in early June.

11 Croxley men lost their lives during the Spring Offensive.

---

### 'Missing in Action' - Edgar Toms - a family's anxious search for news

Edgar Toms joined up in June 1916 at the age of eighteen. He spent eleven months training near Edinburgh and joined the Royal Sussex Regiment as a signaller at the Front in May 1917. He was wounded soon afterwards and then, after recuperating, he retrained as an artillery observer. By 25 January 1918 he had taken up his new job with 24th Observation Group of the 5th Field Survey Company of the Royal Engineers. The job of the Field Survey units was to locate enemy artillery and provide maps and target information to the British gunners.[96]

95. *Little Folks* was a popular children's magazine at the time.
96 See 'The Field Survey Units, R. E. 1914-18' on The Long, Long Trail website. (1914-1918.net/re_survey.htm)

*Edgar Toms (second row from back, fourth from left) with some of his Royal Fusiliers training battalion in Scotland, 1916*

As commonly happened, moving up into the front line was not a straightforward business. 'I have been on the move ever since I left the school last Sunday week, with the exception of a few days' rest at certain places. We spent two nights (last Sunday and Monday) in a cattle truck travelling on the railway. After the way of the Army we travelled a long way round to come a comparatively short distance. On Tuesday morning we landed in a muddy French village which, I am told, is about 40 miles behind the line... We are billeted in an empty house, somewhat dilapidated but still fairly comfortable. In our back garden, by the way, we have a little souvenir in the shape of an unexploded aerial torpedo, probably dropped when this place was nearer to the front line than it is now.'[97]  A couple of weeks later he was still in the same place and commented, 'I am sorry to hear that you get so many air raids, but luckily you are well out of London and are merely lookers-on. We also frequently have visits of enemy aircraft at night over here. In fact only a few evenings ago several bombs were dropped round about our billet, one dropping only about forty yards away. Now we sit on the "qui vive" every evening and you ought to see the way we dive for the dugout at the sound of an enemy plane!'.[98]

A couple of weeks later Edgar wrote home, 'At present I am on a rather quiet part of the front, though whether it will get livelier in future I cannot say, but I should be quite contented if it were even quieter than it is now! Just lately I have passed away several evenings off duty in playing chess....I didn't know anything about chess before I came here, and having won a game the other evening (the only game I have ever won in my life) I am looking to be a champion some day!'.[99] The last letter his parents

97. Letter from Edgar Toms, 25 January, 1918.
98. Letter from Edgar Toms, 14 February 1918
99. Letter from Edgar Toms, 26 February 1918

received was dated 9 March 1918. He commented on delays in the post from England (which was not unusual). He did not write about his own situation but responded to news from home. 'I am pleased that you enjoyed the little tea party mentioned in your letter. I suppose the rationing scheme will spoil those little pleasures unless you take your ration with you when you go out to tea. However, I expect you will be much better off as regards food by now....' His mother's reply, dated 21 March, was returned to Hollybank, Yorke Road, stamped 'address unknown', 'location uncertain'. In it she wrote that she hoped he had received the parcel she sent, and commented, 'Flowers and things in the garden tell us that spring is here and the weather is lovely. If only the war was over, how we should enjoy it.... Mr Wilson gave me quite a nice little bunch of rhubarb on Saturday, so that reminds us of spring too'.

*Edgar Toms (left) with colleagues in Scotland 1917*

Soon afterwards, Edgar's parents knew that the military situation was going very badly for the British Army. As became clear from subsequent correspondence, Edgar had been located just behind the front line south of St Quentin, on the southern edge of the German onslaught on 21 March 1918.

Not having heard from Edgar for several weeks, his father, William Toms, wrote and received a reply from Second Lieutenant G Banes Condy of 24th Observation Group dated 19 April. Condy was not able to provide much information. Edgar had been on duty with another man in a strong point near the front line. They had been unable to get back through German shellfire. Condy thought they must either have been killed or taken prisoner. He emphasised that the enemy <u>was</u> taking prisoners, as one of his men was taken and escaped. Soon afterwards, and in common with many other parents at this time, William and Lizzie received the formal news from the Army Record Office that Sapper E J Toms was posted as 'missing' on 21 March 1918.[100] The German advance had been so rapid that some 90,000 British soldiers were taken prisoner in the Spring Offensive overall.

100. Army Form B. 104-83, 21 April 1918

William lost no time in making enquiries about Edgar, first with the Red Cross who promised to do what they could to find out more. Then amongst many letters of sympathy from friends and relatives, William and Lizzie received a note from Sergeant William Railton who knew Edgar well, to tell them that he had heard that Edgar had been taken prisoner. One of Edgar's colleagues, Frank Steel, had written to his family to say that on the morning of 21 March they found themselves almost surrounded. They held on until 6.30 in the evening but then the Germans made a bombing raid and those who were not killed were made prisoner. Frank said that he had seen Edgar also a prisoner but became separated from him.[101]

This letter offered real hope that Edgar was alive. Not having heard anything from the Red Cross, William approached the Swiss Legation in London, who suggested that he should try the Bureau International de la Paix, Recherche des Prisonniers de Guerre, Berne.[102] William did so without delay and wrote, 'I trust to your good offices to obtain for us some relief from the long suspense and anxiety'.

Meanwhile, Sergeant Railton made contact again, in a letter dated 17 July to say that he had heard from the father of Sapper Wilfred Lord who had been on duty together with Edgar on 21 March. Mr Lord had written that his son had been taken prisoner and was in Germany. William contacted the Lord family in Todmorden, Yorkshire, for news. They sent a letter from Wilfred dated 10 May, in which he gave his address as 87 Royal Engineers, Kriegsgefangenlager [Prisoner of War camp], Stendal:

> On the Wednesday morning two of us were on duty for our 24 hours and would have been relieved at ten o'clock on the Thursday morning (March 21). But as fate willed it Germany opened her attack on that morning; and it was impossible to relieve us. My chum and I fell in with the infantry and held out all Thursday until about five o'clock on the Friday, when we were rushed by the German troops. It was the first bit of bad luck that has happened to me since I joined the Army and I sincerely hope that the bad luck has finished. Perhaps I should not call it bad luck as many things might have happened that we should prefer this instead of. I am alive and well, and that is something to be thankful for.

William tried writing to Edgar via an address in Germany, on 27 July:

> We are in great distress and anxiety because we do not hear from you. Another member of your group tells us that he has seen you in Germany and we cannot understand why you are not allowed to write, but perhaps you are wounded and cannot write, if so, can you get someone to send us a few words to relieve our suspense. Your anxious father…

Over the next few months, William did all he could think of to find out what had happened. He contacted the International Bureau again, and wrote to Edgar's employers, the Local Government Board, who commented on 24 August that some parents of those reported missing on 21 March had only just received letters. So hope was kept alive. He kept in contact with the Lord family and the Steels but there was

101. Letter from Frank Steel, 20 April 1918
102. The International Peace Bureau, now based in Geneva, was founded in 1891-92 and won the Nobel Peace Prize in 1910. (See www.ipb.org)

still nothing. It was not until 22 November that the Toms family received the news they had been dreading. The International Bureau wrote, 'It is our painful duty to inform you that we got news from the camp of Stendal that Private Edgar Toms died on June 3rd 1918 at the hospital of Flavy-le-Martel'. The German camp where Edgar was held was at Flavy-le-Martel, south west of St Quentin, and not far behind the German front line in June.

Naturally, William and Lizzie Toms were anxious to find out how Edgar had died. Early in 1919, Wilfred Lord was repatriated and wrote to William on 21 January from King George's Hospital, Stamford Street, London. He explained that he and Edgar kept together after they were taken prisoner, when Edgar was taken ill with dysentery and went into the camp hospital on Sunday 26 May. After that Wilfred had seen Edgar for a few moments' chat on several days but the camp moved away on 6 June. 'Edgar was receiving treatment of some kind; good, bad or indifferent I cannot say.' The Toms lost no time in going into London to see Wilfred.

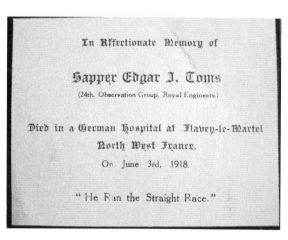

In Affectionate Memory of

**Sapper Edgar J. Toms**

(24th. Observation Group, Royal Engineers.)

Died in a German Hospital at Flavy-le-Martel North West France.

On June 3rd, 1918.

" He Ran the Straight Race. "

*Memorial card sent by William and Lizzie Toms to friends and family*

William informed Sergeant Railton of Edgar's death and asked for further details of where Edgar was when he was taken prisoner. Railton, who was still in France, replied with a long, sympathetic letter dated 7 December 1918:

> The Observation Post where your son was undoubtedly captured was situated in the actual fort at FORT VENDEUIL. Vendeuil is about four miles NW of La Fere and 9 miles south of St Quentin, whence there runs a main road. The fort is constructed of brick, stone and cement and stands on a fairly high contour. It was built, I think, about 1870 or prior. It is just west of the [River] Oise and only a thousand yards from the then front line. The post billet was 500 yds or so behind the fort, wooden shacks on the side of a road. The fort was a very conspicuous landmark and the Hun knew, of course, its value to us. Well immediately the offensive commenced a terrific barrage was put down on our lines and completely encircled the fort. Believe me, nothing could have lived through that. Nobody would attempt to leave the fort....

> That fort held out all day in spite of gas shelling and all the fiendish methods the Hun could think of. I think you will find that the Despatch published by Field Marshal Haig a month or so ago mentions this fort as holding out for two days. Without hope of relief and against tremendous odds those Britishers held on for the sake of their fellows fighting on the wings and in the rear. Those men probably numbering two hundred accounted for many Huns. I do not know

whether they eventually surrendered or were stormed but I do know that your son was in the fort and would take his share with the others....

I only hope that you may be able to get further news as to the cause of your son's death. The Younger report leaves no doubt as to the vileness of the Hun and prisoners recently liberated will have something to say.[103] It may be that some of those may have a message for you.

Believe me Mr Toms, the men out here <u>know</u> the Hun and there is no pity in their hearts. There is no need to dwell on recent events or to tell you how fully we have avenged the March affair, but I would to God that we could visit upon the Huns something in proportion to what they have caused our men to suffer. Well, the future is not yet absolutely settled, but if the Hun tries any tricks he is in for a taste of hell itself.

It took until the end of January 1919 for formal confirmation of Edgar's death from dysentery to arrive from the British Army, along with the usual message of sympathy from the King and Queen, signed by the Secretary of State for War, Winston Churchill.

Edgar Toms is buried in the hospital cemetery at Annois with 61 others. His gravestone bears the inscription chosen by his parents, 'He ran the straight race'.

During these months the *Observer's* columns recorded long lists of casualties. On 11 April Field Marshal Haig issued his famous special order, 'There is no other course open to us but to fight it out. Every position must be held to the the the last man; there must be no retirement. With our backs to the wall and believing in the justice of our cause each one of us must fight on to the end.'[104] The *Observer's* Editor reflected that the 'news may be black but we know we shall win through to victory in the end' (*WO* 13 April 1918). On 27 April, he referred to the casualties of the Hertfordshire and Bedfordshire regiments as 'heroes all' and exhorted readers to do their bit by making use of waste materials. The Watford firm of Geo Ausden, still a

103. Report of Justice Younger's report on the treatment of Prisoners of War in Germany issued 14 October 1918.
104. Field Marshal Sir Douglas Haig, Special Order of the Day Thursday April 11th 1918.

familiar name locally today, followed up with advertisements offering to recycle scrap.

The paper included reports of several Croxley men. Private William Chilton, Grenadier Guards, was severely wounded. Also wounded were Arthur Howard, King's Royal Rifle Corps (45 New Road), A Ford, King's Liverpool Regiment and Sergeant A Owen Royal Garrison Artillery (32 New Road). Henry Owen, Grenadier Guards (147 New Road) was seriously wounded, losing his left leg and two fingers. He had been in France since August 1914, and was wounded in the head in the first Battle of Ypres and again in October 1915. His last four Christmases were spent in France. Private H W Seabrook, Essex Regiment, of New Road, who had previously been reported missing, had written saying he was a prisoner of war. The *Observer* reported that the Military Medal had been awarded to Corporal William George Dorrofield, King's Royal Rifle Corps (246 New Road) Richard Henry Hopkins Royal Naval Division (120 New Road) and Corporal Robert Charles Siggers, Royal Engineers (303 New Road).

All Saints' Church Easter Vestry meeting also considered the war. The war shrine had been updated to include 340 names, of whom 34 had been killed, 54 wounded and 4 taken prisoner. Charles Barton-Smith was again elected people's warden and A C Rickett was nominated as the vicar's warden.

There was tragic news from the home front during April. An unidentified new born baby girl was found dead in the canal near Croxley Mills after 14 days in the water. The inquest verdict was death due to neglect at the time of birth (*WO* 13 April 1918). A labourer at Croxley Mills, Charles Barnett from the Mill Cottages Cassiobridge, fell down a coal shute and was suffocated by coal falling on top of him (*WO* 27 April and 4 May 1918).

The Government made a big effort to sell war bonds to finance the war. Watford received a visit from a tank known as 'Julian'. The *Observer* reported on 11 May that the Tank Week celebrations had been reminiscent of pre-war days with displays of flags, a long procession and the streets crowded with enthusiastic people. It made a welcome change from the drab pre-occupations and anxieties of the war. The tank's visit was complemented by a couple of aeroplanes performing graceful and daring aerobatics. £72,000 was subscribed in two days.

### Farewell to the Parish Nurse

But the war did not dominate everything in the village. There was still room for the important kindnesses of life. In May, a presentation was organised for Nurse Warters who had been the parish nurse for four years. She was taking up a similar post at Croxley Mills. The event took place in the grounds of Briery Close (by kind invitation of Miss Barker). Over 500 subscribers contributed to the gifts of an illuminated certificate, a book containing the names of the subscribers, a clock and a cheque for £30 2s 6d. The vicar, Rev Blois Bisshopp, said that she had earned the love of all, not only by her great skill, but by her unfailing sympathy and cheerfulness. Nurse Warters, her bicycle, her little black bag, and her smile were familiar to all. She had never spared herself, but had given of her best to all who needed her services. He

# CROXLEY MEN KILLED IN THE 1918 SPRING OFFENSIVE

Albert Allaway, Stanley Beament and Francis Thomas all died on 21 March and they are all remembered on the Pozieres memorial, at the Somme. Altogether, 11 Croxley men were killed.

**Private Albert Allaway**, 24th Battalion, Machine Gun Corps, was 24 when he died. He was the husband of E M Allaway, 38 Copsewood Road, Watford. He originally enlisted in the Yorkshire Regiment. In 1911, Albert lived with his parents, William and Charlotte, at Croxley Mill Cottages. His father worked as a boilerman at the mill, while Albert was a labourer in a brickyard. He is listed on the Dickinson memorial, so must have become a mill worker later.

**Rifleman Stanley William Beament**, served in D Company, 9th Battalion, King's Royal Rifle Corps and was 20 when he died. He had been wounded twice previously. Stanley was born in Croxley on 26 September 1897, to William and Fanny Beament of 123 New Road. He was one of nine children. Like his older brother Jack, Stanley had been a member of the Church Lads' Brigade, but Stanley enlisted later and so ended up in a different Battalion of the KRRC. He is also listed on the Dickinson memorial.

**Private Francis Albert Thomas**, 2nd Battalion Bedfordshire Regiment, was 32 when he died. Frank's chaplain was quoted in the *Observer* of 27 April, 'He died as a fine soldier, doing his duty bravely and well to the last. We honour his memory for his fine and noble example'. In 1911, Frank was living with his parents (Francis Albert senior and Elizabeth Ann Thomas) at 112 New Road. It was a big family. His mother had 12 children of whom 9 survived. His father was a papermaker and Frank was a clerk at Croxley Mills.

**Lance Corporal Arthur John Owen**, 16th (The Queen's) Lancers, died on 26 March, aged 23. He is also remembered at Pozieres. In 1911, Arthur was living with his parents (Thomas and Alice) at 7 Cassiobridge Terrace. His father was a domestic gardener and Arthur worked as a shop assistant. His mother had 12 children of whom 10 survived. According to the *Observer* of 27 April, he was born at Croxley Green, went to school there and afterwards at Chater School, Watford. He worked as a motor driver at the Watford Co-operative Society and joined the Army a year before the war broke out, leaving for France two years later. His Captain, writing to his father, said that he was a great loss to the Regiment as he had done magnificently and would certainly have been recommended for quick promotion. His gallantry and contempt for death were encouraging to the men. He died leading his men to stop the enemy, who had temporarily broken through the line. In 1918, Thomas and Alice Owen were registered at Cassiobridge House. The *Observer* added that the Owens had two other sons (Edward and Frank) and two sons-in-law serving in the forces.

**Private Lewis John Dean**, 2nd Battalion, Suffolk Regiment, died on 28 March. He would have been about 32 years old and is buried at Souchez, near Lens. He was formerly in the Bedfordshire Regiment. In 1911, Lewis was living with his parents, John and Isabella, at 1 Briery Close Cottages, Croxley Green. He was a labourer and his father worked for the County Council as a roadman.

**Private Sidney Albert Element**, 2nd Battalion Middlesex Regiment, died on 24 April 1918. He was buried at Villers-Bretonneux, where the German advance was halted, east of Amiens. Sidney was 11 at the time of the 1911 census, so he would have been about 18 when he died. According to All Saints' shrine he enlisted in 1917 when he would have been under age. Sidney was the eldest son of Herbert and Eliza Element. They kept a greengrocer's and confectioner's shop and lived at 22 New Road.

**Private Charles Webb**, 5th Battalion Middlesex Regiment, died on 11 May, aged 31. According to Neil Wheeler he died in Croxley Green but the circumstances of his death are not known. He is buried in Chorleywood Road cemetery, Rickmansworth. Charles was the son of Joseph Webb and the husband of Fanny Elizabeth Webb of 267 New Road. On census day in 1911, Charles and Elizabeth were living with their son Joseph as boarders at 18 Manor Cottages, The Swillet, Chorleywood. In 1911 Charles was working as a domestic chauffeur. He is listed on the Dickinson memorial.

**Corporal Edwin Frederick Mead**, 18th Battalion King's Royal Rifle Corps, died of wounds on 23 May, aged 20. He is buried at Esquelbecq military cemetery, between Dunkirk and St Omer. Edwin was the third son of George and Fanny Mead of 179 New Road. They also had a daughter. In 1911 George worked as a labourer at the mill and Edwin joined him there later. Edwin's older brother Ernest was killed in May 1917.

**Private Arthur Baylis Pargeter**, 4th Battalion Machine Gun Corps, died on 31 May, aged 28. He is buried at Etaples military cemetery. Etaples is near the French coast, south of Boulogne, where many hospitals were located during the war. Arthur was the son of Albert and Mary Pargeter of Mount Pleasant, Yorke Road. In 1911 the family lived on Scots Hill and in 1901 in Rickmansworth High Street. Albert was a drayman and Arthur an office boy. They both worked at a brewery.

**Sapper Edgar John Toms**, see main text.

**Lance-Corporal John Josiah Revell**, 1st Battalion Dorsetshire Regiment, died on 19 June, aged about 31. He was buried at Berles new military cemetery, south west of Arras. John was born in Croxley, the son of Henry Revell and the family lived in Copthorne Cottages on the Green. In 1911 Henry was a widower and gave his occupation as a bricklayer. John was a garden labourer. Henry had 12 children of whom 9 were still living in 1911. John is listed on the Dickinson memorial.

was sure that the ray of sunshine she left with her patients often did them quite as much good as the doctor's medicine. The meeting closed with cheers for Nurse Warters and singing of the National Anthem (*WO* 1 June 1918).

A couple of similar events took place in July. At Croxley Mills, on Friday 5 July, Francis Albert Thomas (of 112 New Road) was presented by the staff with a handsome armchair and umbrella, on the occasion of his retirement from the service of Messrs John Dickinson & Co. [Francis had just suffered the loss of his son in the war.] Charles Barton-Smith, said that Mr Thomas had been with the firm for 33 years, and in his position as Head Finisher in the Writings Department had enhanced the reputation of the firm as makers of good quality writing papers (*WO* 13 July 1918).

At the quarterly meeting of the United Patriots' Benefit Society on 13 July, the Chairman, Mr Sam Hussey (of 5 Dickinson Square), was presented by the members with an (inscribed) walking stick, a case of briar pipes and tobacco. Mr Barton-Smith made the presentation and complimented Mr Hussey on the way he had steered the Society so harmoniously during his 20 years as chairman (*WO* 20 July 1918).

By August the war had been dragging on for four years and a national day of remembrance was arranged. In Watford a united service took place at the West Herts ground and, in Rickmansworth, the day was observed by the churches (*WO* 10 August 1918). But all was not sweetness and light on the home front. The newspaper reported that there were no Bakerloo trains at the end of August because the women workers, who were keeping the tube running, had gone on strike (*WO* 31 August 1918).

*Church Lads' Brigade band (about 1914). Cyril Toms third from right in back row.*

*Croxley Green Church Lads at camp in Latimer in 1913. Photo signed ABS (Arthur Barton-Smith)*

The Croxley Green Church Lads' Brigade kept up their tradition of a summer camp in Latimer (*WO* 17 August 1918). This year they joined forces with companies from Rickmansworth, Watford, St. Albans and Abbots Langley. The Croxley contingent marched to Latimer to set up camp. Over the following week, the lads took part in church parade at Chenies, a route march, drill, a shooting competition, cricket and sports. The Croxley company distinguished themselves. Denton and Hawtin from Croxley won the shooting and Croxley won the best kept tent and the tug-of-war. Camp management was in the capable hands of Sergeant Major T Denton.

John Gudgin joined the camp as an instructor. As a youngster, he was the band sergeant of the Croxley Company, and he enlisted with the 16th KRRC as soon as he was able in January 1916. He had been seriously wounded at High Wood in July that year and was discharged on medical grounds in June 1917. Gudgin instructed the bugle band at camp and organised and conducted the shooting competition.

During this last phase of the war the Observer continued reporting on the fortunes of Croxley men:

> - Lieutenant S Ashby, son of Mr and Mrs William Ashby of 266 New Road was gazetted captain in the South Wales Borderers (*WO* 31 August 1918)
> - Lance-Corporal J D Hull, 2/15th London Regiment, was awarded the Military Medal. He was the second son of Harry Hull of 36 New Road. He had been a member of the Church Lads and then the King's Royal Rifle Corps (*WO* 28 September 1918).

The list of the wounded recorded by the *Observer* included: G Chapman, Royal Lancaster Regiment (reported 28 September); Jack Beament, King's Royal Rifles, of 123 New Road, wounded for the third time and progressing satisfactorily in hospital

# THE ALLIES ADVANCE TO VICTORY ON THE WESTERN FRONT

The Allied counter-attack, now including a growing American presence, began with the second battle of the Marne on 18 July. This turned the tide of German advance. On 8 August the British and French armies launched a decisive assault along the Somme towards Peronne. The German commander, Ludendorff, referred to this as 'the black day of the German army'. By the beginning of September the Allies had forced the Germans back to the positions they had occupied before the Spring Offensive. On 29 September the Allies broke through the heavily fortified German defences at the Hindenburg line and pursued the retreating German armies eastwards. This phase from August to October involved some of the hardest fighting of the war and British casualties exceeded 300,000. 5 more Croxley men were killed.

*British troops with flags and flowers at the liberation of Lille*

# CROXLEY MEN KILLED ON THE WESTERN FRONT - JULY TO NOVEMBER 1918

**Private James Revell**, 1st Battalion Herefordshire Regiment, 34th Division, died on 23 July and is remembered at Villemontoire cemetery, south of Soissons. The cemetery is connected with the victorious advance of the 15th (Scottish) and 34th Divisions from 23 July to 2 August. James was the older brother of John Revell who died the month before. James would have been about 32 when he died. In 1911 he was working as a paper mill labourer but he is not listed on the Dickinson memorial.

**Private Albert Goddard**, 1st/1st Battalion, Cambridgeshire Regiment, died on 5 September. According to the *Observer* of 5 October, he was killed by machine gun fire when attacking with his company. The paper reported that he had been in France two years and previously worked for a building firm in Watford. He is buried at Peronne, Somme. Albert was 38 when he died. He lived with his wife Louisa and four children at 171 New Road. In 1911, he was a labourer at the paper mill but is also not listed on the Dickinson memorial. He came originally from Wiltshire.

**Private Alfred Albert Pettifer**, 9th Battalion Royal Fusiliers (City of London Regiment), died 21 September. He is buried at Epehy Wood between Cambrai and Peronne in the Somme. He was born in Croxley on 19 February 1898. His parents were James and Harriet Pettifer, who lived at 7 Croxley Mill Cottages, Cassiobridge. In 1911 James worked as a storekeeper at the mill.

**Lance-Corporal Joseph Woollams**, 4th Battalion Bedfordshire Regiment, died on 30 September. He is remembered on the memorial to the missing at Vis-en-Artois, east of Arras. He was born on 9 March 1893, so would have been 25 when he died. Joseph was the eldest of the seven children (in 1911) of Joseph and Mary Rose Woollams of 231 New Road. His brother William was killed in March 1917. Joseph and Mary Rose were married on 15 October 1893. In 1911 Joseph senior worked as a labourer at the paper mill and Joseph junior worked as a labourer on a farm. The family and his sweetheart, Dolly, placed a moving memorial notice in the *Observer*'s columns.

**Sergeant William George Dorrofield MM**, 13th Battalion King's Royal Rifle Corps, died of wounds on 4 November 1918. He is remembered at Romeries, near Solesmes, east of Cambrai. He would have been about 20 when he died. William was the second of the seven children (in 1911) of William and Rose Charlotte Dorrofield. The family lived at 246 New Road and William senior was a water cress grower.

in Nottingham (reported 16 November); C W Seabrook, Lancashire Fusiliers, and J Webb, East Yorks Regiment, (both reported 16 November); and Corporal Victor Duncombe, 1st Royal Scots Fusiliers (259 New Road, reported 21 December). Gunner Lewis Arthur Ford, Royal Field Artillery, (198 New Road) was reported taken prisoner on 30 November. (News of prisoners of war often took many weeks to arrive.)

By 5 October the fighting was going much better for the Allies and the editor of the *Observer* was able to write a leading article with the title, 'Victory in the Air'. People in Croxley Green were probably feeling a bit more optimistic too. It had been a good harvest and All Saint's church was beautifully decorated for the harvest festival on the last Sunday in September. At the close of evensong a solemn Te Deum of Thanksgiving was sung and it was dedicated to the deliverance of the Holy Land from Turkish rule.

# ALLIED VICTORY OVER TURKEY

In 1918 the British Expeditionary Force in Mesopotamia built on its success in capturing Baghdad in 1917 and pushed northwest up the Tigris and Euphrates. In Palestine, British forces had captured Jerusalem in December 1917 and rapidly advanced northwards, reaching Aleppo by the end of October 1918. Meanwhile, the Turks took advantage of the collapse of the Russian army to attack Armenia and invade north eastern Persia. Persia was nominally neutral but parts of the country were garrisoned by both Russia and Britain. The British forces resisted the Turkish invasion. In the face of defeat in Palestine and Mesopotamia, the Turks surrendered to the British on 30 October.

**Driver John Henry Newberry**, 386th Battery, Royal Field Artillery, died on 25 August 1918, aged 21. He is remembered on the Tehran memorial in Iran. John was the son of Matthew and Jane Newberry of the Duke of York public house on Watford Road. According to the *Observer* of 14 September, he died of colitis. John had been a choirboy at St. Mary's Rickmansworth and, before joining the army worked for a printing company in Watford. John's brother Samuel had been killed in November 1917. In 1911 the Newberry family lived at 66 Church Street, Rickmansworth. Matthew was a steam crane driver for a gravel company and John, aged 13, was a newsboy at the railway bookstall. Matthew and Jane Newberry had 13 children of whom 9 survived (in 1911).

## Influenza pandemic

The end of the war may have been in sight but there was a new worry, a severe outbreak of influenza, which had started in the trenches of France in spring 1918. At first it took a mild form but, by the summer, many sufferers developed complications and a high proportion of those affected died. Some historians have estimated the worldwide death toll by late 1919 as up to 70 million people.[105] More American servicemen died of influenza than were killed in battle.[106]

---

# INFLUENZA - CROXLEY GREEN MILITARY DEATHS

**Private Lionel Aslin Peek**, 53rd Battalion, Middlesex Regiment, died of pneumonia at Connaught Hospital, Aldershot on 24 October 1918, aged 18. He was born in Croxley on 3 August 1900, the son of Arthur James and Susan Maria Axtel Peek of 196 New Road. In 1911 both Lionel's father and his eldest brother worked at Croxley Mills. Lionel himself is listed on the Dickinson memorial so it seems he followed in his father's footsteps.

The *Observer* of 2 November reported his burial, with military honours, which took place on 30 October at Rickmansworth Cemetery in Chorleywood Road. According to the report, the body was borne from All Saints' church to the cemetery on a gun carriage. The Rev Blois Bisshopp officiated at a service that was very well attended. Many people left beautiful floral tributes. The Croxley Green Volunteers, under Sergeant Beck, fired the salute over the grave and the 'Last Post' was played. Lionel was a popular member of the Church Lads' Brigade and Village Football Club, who was esteemed for his large heartedness and enthusiasm.

**Air Mechanic John Belgrove Sirett** may well have been another victim of influenza, although no precise evidence has been found. He died on 2 November while he was based at Eastchurch airfield in Kent with the 58th Training Wing of the newly formed Royal Air Force. He was 30 when he died, the son of John Edward and Mary Sirett of 219 New Road. In 1918 he was living at 1 Watford Road. John married Dorothy Elizabeth Batchelor in 1914 and they had two daughters, Doris and Winifred. In 1923, Dorothy married Francis O'Mahony and they lived at 15, Gonville Avenue, Croxley Green. John is also buried in Chorleywood Road Cemetery. The grave inscription uses the phrase 'who passed away November 2nd 1918', which suggests death from illness rather than in conflict. In 1911 John Sirett was a carpenter and joiner living with his parents at 219 New Road. His father was a dairyman and the family had come from Wandsworth.

---

105. Simon Forty, *World War One, A Visual Encyclopedia,* PRC Publishing 2002, p. 203
106. Martin Gilbert, *First World War,* Weidenfield and Nicholson 1994, p. 540

According to the *Observer* of 2 November, an outbreak began locally about the beginning of October and had caused such concern that all the schools were closed from the middle of the month. In bad cases the influenza led to pneumonia, which could be fatal in a few days. For the three weeks ending 19 October only 8 deaths occurred in Watford. In the three days, 26, 27 and 28 October, there were some 15 fatal cases and after that the daily death rate in Watford had been about 7. The local Medical Officer had advised that the schools should remain closed for at least another fortnight and had arranged for the treatment of severe cases in a ward in the Isolation Hospital.

Rickmansworth was also seriously affected. There were as many as 7 deaths in the Urban District Council area in the last week of October. The *Observer* reported that there were difficulties in preparing graves. In one case, an undertaker had to dig one himself for lack of labour. Influenza was responsible for the death of at least two Croxley servicemen, Lionel Peek and Sir Guy Calthrop, and probably a third, John Sirett. On 9 November, the *Observer* reported that, for the third week the schools in the District had been closed by the order of the Deputy Medical Officer (Dr Evans) owing to the prevalence of influenza. The log book of Croxley Girls' School records that the school was closed from 22 October until 11 November 1918.

**All Saints' Memorial Service**

Rev Blois Bisshopp led the congregation at All Saints' in a memorial service for the 44 Croxley Green men who were then recognised as having died on active service. As in previous years, the service was held on All Souls' day, 2 November (*WO* 9 November 1918). The vicar said that, through their sorrow for these heroes, everyone felt pride that in the hour of their country's need they had not been found wanting. They could never forget them. He continued that thanksgiving was a ray of light, because death was not the end, and love must one day be crowned by reunion. The service ended with the National Anthem and the Dead March played by the organist, William Acton Gittins, followed by the 'Last Post' played by Messrs Gudgin and Hunt.

**The Armistice**

As in the rest of the country, news of Germany's signing of the Armistice was met with scenes of rejoicing in West Herts on Monday 11 November (*WO* 16 November 1918). There was no doubt that Britain had achieved a great victory. Soon after 9 am, factories in Watford sounded their hooters, people came out onto the streets and the atmosphere was festive. Buildings were decorated with Union Jacks and the streets with bunting. Flags were everywhere. Girls from the munition works danced in the market place and even the afternoon drizzle failed to dampen public enthusiasm. At nightfall, the street lamps shone out for the first time since the beginning of the winter of 1915. The gloom of the past four years had disappeared as if by magic. Little work was done during the day but according to the local police, the crowds behaved well and there was not a single case of drunkenness.

Similar celebrations took place in Rickmansworth and Croxley Green with flags, bunting and church bells ringing out. There was a bonfire in Rickmansworth High

*(Above) Croxley schoolchildren celebrate the Armistice in Dickinson Square.
(Below) Patients and staff outside the Dickinson Institute mark Armistice day.
Photos from the Hospital Quartermaster's autograph book.*

Street and a fireworks display. At Croxley Girls' School everyone commenced work on Monday 11 November after returning from the long enforced absence caused by influenza. Then the head mistress recorded, 'hearing the Peace Bells we distributed our flags, formed into procession with the Infants and Boys and went to the Church outside which we sang God save the King. We went to the hospital and several of the wounded men made short speeches, also Mr Kennedy. Then after giving lusty cheers we went round the village'.[107] All Saints' church put on a thanksgiving service for victory at 8 pm. The building was filled to capacity. Many were standing and many failed to get inside. Wounded soldiers from the local VAD hospital were conspicuous in the congregation. The vicar, Rev Blois Bisshopp, gave thanks for victory and preached on the text, 'Sing unto the Lord for he has triumphed gloriously; the horse and his rider hath He thrown into the sea'.[108] He emphasised the glorious achievements of the Army and Navy and the incessant prayers of people at home. Then on Tuesday 12 November all the schoolchildren went to church as an act of thanksgiving for the hope of peace.

Almost lost in the attention given to the end of the war was the announcement of the death of Robert Grosvenor, the Second Lord Ebury, in his 85th year, on 13 November. This presaged a major change locally since the heir, Robert Victor Grosvenor, decided to put Moor Park estate up for sale. It was purchased in September 1919 by the industrialist, Lord Leverhulme (*WO* 14 December 1918).

**General Election**

No sooner was the ink on the Armistice document dry than the political elite started preparing for the postponed national election. The local M P, Arnold Ward, had resigned after returning from his war service. The contest was between Dennis Herbert, a Unionist representing Lloyd George's governing coalition, Frank Gray, a private soldier representing the Liberal party, and George Lathan for the Labour party. The voting lists now included women aged over 30 and men aged over 21. According to the *Observer*, there were 32,801 electors on the register for the Watford Division compared with 18,454 in 1910 when the Liberals came a close second. In 1918, there were 900 electors in Croxley Green who were invited to vote at the Boys' and Girls' Schools (*WO* 14 December 1918). For comparison, there were 2,148 electors in Rickmansworth and 16,994 in Watford. Croxley Green was similar in size to Chorleywood. Of course, those still on war service had to be added to those numbers. The absentee voters amounted to 27 per cent of those resident in the district. This gives some idea of the large proportion of the local population who were involved in war service in 1918.

Closer scrutiny of the register for Croxley Green reveals that there were 1,167 people qualified to vote. This number includes 26 from Croxley Mill cottages which were in the separate polling district of Rickmansworth Rural. 483 (41%) of the electors were women and most qualified to vote because of their husband's occupation. 265 (23%

107 Croxley Green National School log book November 1918.
108. Exodus chapter 15 verse 1 - the reference is to the drowning of the Pharaoh's army in the Red Sea when the Israelites made good their escape from slavery in Egypt.

- all men) qualified as voters because of their military service rather than their residence or occupation.

The list of absent voters for Croxley Green has 274 names of servicemen, almost a quarter of the total electors. 14 of them were killed between registration and the end of the war. The majority served in the Army and their units ranged across the spectrum from infantry, artillery and engineers to service, medical and veterinary corps and labour companies. 11 were in the Navy, 20 in the RAF and 5 in the British Red Cross. Only 19 were officers and five of those came from two families: the Agnews of Durrants house (Hugh was a Lieutenant and William a Sub-Lieutenant, both in the Navy), and the Tussauds of 17 New Road (Guy and Hugh were Lieutenants in the RAF and Bernard a Second-Lieutenant in the Machine Gun Corps). The highest ranking serviceman was Lieutenant-Colonel Humphry Stephen Woolrych who was working at the Embarkation Staff in Southampton. Woolrych had succeeded his uncle William as one of the principal land owners in Croxley Green and qualified to vote on the basis of his property. After the war he came to live at Parrotts farm on the Green. 66 names do not appear on All Saints' shrine so the total of Croxley men who served in the military during the war was well over 400.

The election result was a thumping victory for Herbert, the Coalition candidate. He won by over 6,000 votes. Labour came second, pushing the Liberals into an ignominious third place. The turn out was about 60 per cent.

It was hardly surprising that the *Observer's* retrospective on 1918 was much more upbeat than a year earlier (*WO* 28 December 1918). The paper hailed the year of victory and emphasised the strong contribution made by people from West Herts, listing the losses suffered and medals gained by local servicemen.

# 1919

The Armistice was not the end of the war. Final peace terms remained to be settled and the armed forces had to ensure the terms of the ceasefire were kept. Consequently, demobilisation was a slow process. Nevertheless, the *Observer* was able to remark that the Christmas and New Year period had been a real 'khaki holiday' with many troops home on leave (*WO* 4 January 1919).

*The hospital Quartermaster, May Barton-Smith, and patients.*

## Croxley Green VAD Hospital

The work of the VAD hospitals was brought to a close. The Rickmansworth and Croxley Green hospitals closed around the turn of the year. In Croxley, the VAD staff and volunteers were invited to a celebratory supper in the Dickinson Institute on 27 December 1918. 62 people attended. The Commandant, Mrs Kennedy, was unwell but wrote to thank everyone for their hard work during the two and a half years of the hospital's existence (*WO* 4 January 1919). Later, in May, the Hertfordshire Red Cross held a festival in St Albans to celebrate the 30,000 men who passed through the county's VAD hospitals during the war (*WO* 24 May 1919). According to *War Time in a Paper Mill*, the figure for the Croxley hospital, with its 50 beds, was 1,175 patients: an impressive number.

*Hospital patients (above) outside the Dickinson Institute and (below) on the green with Bruce the mascot.*

The last word on the Croxley Green hospital should remain with one of the patients. Arthur Hall Fitzpatrick of the Manchester Regiment wrote the following verse 'In Loving Remembrance of My Short Stay at Croxley':

Our Commandant's a Lady whom everyone admires
And to see Tommy's happy is all her heart desires.
Our Treasurer is Mr Barton Smith, I'm sure you'll all agree
We couldn't get a better if we travelled o'er the sea.
Our cook Mrs Dyde is famous for making good things
And the dishes she puts before us are fit for any King.
Our Quartermaster's a fine one and Boys you do well to grin
For though you get good rations you get plenty buckshee given in.
Mr Heckford is a soldier's Friend of good old fashioned kind
He amuses and instructs us, and the trouble he does not mind.
All our Sisters and our Nurses, well they are just it.
And if they keep a tight hand o'er us I don't mind one bit
So good bye to Croxley Hospital, I felt I ought to say
I hope that I am soon wounded and come for another stay.

Fitzpatrick was killed in action on 2 September 1918 and is buried at Caterpillar Valley cemetery, Longueval, Somme.

*Captain Frank Barton-Smith MC*

### Charles Barton-Smith retires

At Croxley Mills it was the end of an era. Charles Barton-Smith retired as General Manager after 48 years working for John Dickinson and Co Ltd. He had been a manager at the London office for 17 years before becoming manager at Croxley for 23 years. Mr Coutts, the cashier, made the presentation of some antique furniture, commenting on the changes that had taken place during his tenure and the way in which he had ensured there had been no labour troubles during his time (*WO* 4 January 1919).

However, that did not mean Barton-Smith would give up his other duties. He was re-elected Chairman and Secretary of the Dickinson Institute in January, re-elected as an Urban District Councillor in April and re-elected as the people's churchwarden at All Saints' in May

*May, Charles, Maud and Frank Barton-Smith at the Palace*

(*WO* 11 January 1919). He also presided at a meeting to promote membership in Croxley Green of the National Federation of Discharged and Demobilised Soldiers and Sailors. One of the speakers said that they wished to avoid 'Bolshevism' and this could be done by meeting together about any grievances and hearing both sides before any drastic action was taken (*WO* 25 January 1919).

The Barton-Smith family were particularly pleased when their son, Captain Frank Barton-Smith, received his Military Cross from the King in June. It was awarded for distinguished service and leadership in the Somme battles (*WO* 25 January 1919).

A real effort was made to get Croxley's social life back to normal. The engineers at Croxley Mills revived their annual New Year's Ball after a gap for the war years with Mr A Beck as master of ceremonies (*WO* 11 January 1919). Dickinson's hosted a party for some 350 children of Croxley Mills' employees and the Dickinson Institute reopened with a social evening, and then the first weekly dance of the season (*WO* 18 January 1919). The Old Girls of All Saints' School [i.e. Croxley Girls'] held a party too (*WO* 25 January 1919).

As the demobilised troops gradually made their way home, organisations on the Home Front marked the end of their war operations. The Croxley Green local platoon of the Volunteer Training Corps met for a 'smoking concert' at the Dickinson Institute in March to honour their Lieutenant, Maurice Walter Raggett. Sergeant A Beck presided and Corporal Dawes made the presentation (WO 15 March 1919). At least one of Croxley's returned soldiers found it difficult adjusting to civilian ways. Sidney King of Lawn Villa was caught by the long arm of the law and fined 2s 6d for riding his bike without lights. He pleaded ignorance of the law (*WO* 8 November 1919).

*Sir Guy Spencer Calthrop Bart., General Manager of the London and North Western Railway and Government Coal Controller*

# Death of Sir Guy Spencer Calthrop Bart.

Croxley Green lost a distinguished resident, Sir Guy Spencer Calthrop (1870-1919), who died on 23 February, from pneumonia aged 48. He was another victim of the influenza pandemic. Guy Calthrop was the youngest son of Everard Calthrop of Swinehead Abbey, Lincolnshire. His elder brother Everard (1857-1927) became a prominent railway engineer. Guy followed in his footsteps and joined the London and North Western Railway in 1886. He worked his way up through the company and then moved to Scotland in 1901 to become general manager of the Caledonian Railway. In 1910 he moved to Argentina to run the Buenos Aires and Pacific Railway just as the rail link from Argentina across the Andes to the Pacific coast of Chile was completed. Then he returned to Britain as general manager of the London and North Western Railway in 1914.

Towards the end of 1916 the Government gradually increased its control of the economy in support of the war effort. In the autumn, as South Wales miners threatened to disrupt the vital coal supply, the industry was placed under state control. Guy Calthrop was given the job of managing the situation as Controller of Coal Mines in February 1917. He negotiated with both sides of the industry to increase production and appears to have earned the respect of mine-owners and miners' leaders. The miners gained higher pay and the industry remained very profitable thanks to a guaranteed market, even if prices were controlled. Production in 1916 was higher than the year before but, in the last two years of the war, there was a race between shrinking coal supplies and mounting strategic needs. Calthrop used his railway expertise to reorganise the transportation of coal to avoid unnecessary journeys. Coal rationing was introduced in 1918 and, because of the effort to stockpile fuel during the summer, consumers had better access to coal than in previous winters. (Death of Sir Guy Calthrop, *The Times*, 24 February 1919.)

Calthrop held the rank of Lieutenant Colonel in the Royal Engineers and, as such, is recorded in the list of war dead by the Commonwealth War Graves Commission,

although he is not listed on the Croxley Green memorial. For his war work, Calthrop was created a Baronet in June 1918. He lived with his wife, Gertrude Margaret, for several years at Croxley House. She was the eighth daughter of James Morten of the Savoy, Denham. They had no children. Calthrop's funeral took place on 2 March at All Saints'. A special train was arranged from Euston to Croxley Green. (*The Times,* 28 February, *WO* 9 March 1919.) Gertrude died in 1929 aged 49. They are both buried in a large, unkempt plot, whose cross lies fallen on the grass, in Chorleywood Road cemetery, Rickmansworth.

The war had played a part in bringing people together. One Croxley Green girl, Irene Hawtin of New Road, married a Canadian soldier at All Saints' in January (*WO* 4 January 1919). Then in June, Dorothea Denton, who had been a member of the Women's Auxiliary Army Corps in France, married Captain James Henry Wood OBE of Harlesden. Dorothea had been a member of the Croxley Mills office staff. Her parents, Thomas and Rosa Denton, lived at 36 Dickinson Square (*WO* 28 June 1919).

Dickinson's reinvigorated their sports programme. The Croxley Mills shooting team won the South African Shield at the local range in a contest against Dickinson's London office. Mr A Beck captained the Croxley team and the other members were Thomas Plumridge, Maurice Raggett and Messrs L Chapman, J Hawtin, Bubb, Flitton, Wells, H Holloway and Green (*WO* 21 June 1919). Later in June, Croxley Mills and the London office revived their annual cricket and tennis matches. Afterwards, the participants enjoyed tea, a concert and music for dancing from the Institute Band (*WO* 5 July 1919).

## Peace Celebrations

Meanwhile, in Paris, the peace negotiations, which had been dragging on since January, were reaching their conclusion. The Treaty of Versailles was signed on 28 June between the Allies and Germany. Throughout the country, local committees started organising peace celebrations and south west Herts was no exception. There were special services at All Saints' to mark 'peace Sunday' on 6 July. Then on 19 July the whole country celebrated the end of the war. In Croxley the village procession assembled on the Green. Then, after singing the 'Old Hundredth' and the National Anthem, they set off at 11 am. The procession included a wide range of local organisations: Croxley Mills Fire Brigade, the Church Lads' Brigade, Girl Guides, workers in the VAD Hospital, the Croxley Platoon of the VTC, Special Constables, and representatives of Friendly Societies such as the Foresters, Oddfellows and United Patriots. At the heart of the procession were members of the armed forces, both demobilised and serving. As the authors of the programme put it, the procession included 'a pageant of men and women who have laboured throughout our Country's History for the uplifting of mankind'.[109]  This took the form of groups dressed up to represent periods of British history over the previous 2,000 years. All this was spiced with patriotic flags and the music of two bands (*WO* 26 July 1919). Sports, games and maypole dancing on the Green took place in the afternoon. Mrs C W Kennedy, lately Commandant of the VAD Hospital, presented the prizes and the evening ended with a torchlight parade.

The Girls' School benefited from six weeks summer holiday to celebrate peace. The girls' work before the holidays had to give place to preparing costumes for the pageant on Peace Day. 'Each girl was dressed in the costume of some special history period – and before each group were banners bearing the names of Great Men of the period.' The girls also celebrated by beating the boys at tug-of-war again.[110]

---

109 Programme for the Croxley Green Peace Celebration, All Saints' Archives.
110  Croxley Green National School log book September 1919.

Croxley children taking part in the peace pageant. The top photo includes Arthur Lamsley (seated front row left) and the bottom photo includes Alice Lamsley (second row, second from right). (Right) Douglas Toms carries a banner.

PEACE 1919

July 19th

With the official celebration of Peace tomorrow, the whole of our Country will lay aside the actual horrors and daily anxieties which were directly brought into all our lives by the War.

The Directors and the whole management of the Firm would like to feel that we were all personally associated in the feelings of gladness and relief which are prevalent in all our hearts.

Our Fathers and Sons, Husbands and Brothers, fought side by side — those who remained at home have worked and striven to support the Fighters, and to keep the Institutions and Industries of the Nation alive, and as far as our Factories are concerned all have nobly done their part in both the fighting and the working.

As we have had one common purpose during the War, so we can all be at one in our feelings of pleasure and happiness during the Peace Celebrations.

Our Country, and the Cause it stood for, has triumphed - the future has stern problems which it will tax our united strength to solve.

Let us unite in joy and thankfulness for the Victory achieved and be sure that, with the same united purpose to work as one for the good of the whole, the difficulties and dangers that lie before us in the future will be as victoriously overcome as those whose defeat we are now celebrating.

John Dickinson & Co. Ltd.

*A message to staff from the management of John Dickinson and Co Ltd on the occasion of the peace celebrations, 19 July 1919.*

## Living with the Consequences

Dickinson's management took the opportunity of the peace celebrations to emphasise the sense of common purpose that kept the nation going during the dark days of the war. 'As far as our factories are concerned, all have nobly done their part in both the fighting and the working.' But they also stressed that 'the future has stern problems which it will tax our united strength to solve'.

The war had affected all Croxley's families in one way or another. There was no way to compensate those who had lost a father, brother or son. Yet they were not the only ones who had to deal with the consequences of the war. Many of those men who returned continued to suffer the physical and mental effects. The impact on their families is little recorded. People were anxious to get on with their lives. They hoped for better things but the war cast a long shadow.

One family which faced hardship was the Lamsleys.[111] Harry and Alice Lamsley had moved to Croxley in 1914. He worked at Sun Printers in Watford. They had three young children and lived at 2 Watford Road. Harry volunteered on 27 March 1915, aged 27, and joined the British Expeditionary Force in the 4th Battalion, Grenadier Guards in April 1916. At the Somme, the Guards were involved in heavy fighting, including at a village called Ginchy, where Harry was wounded on 9 September. He received gunshot wounds in the back and right arm. But his health was also affected by heart disease and inflammation of the eyes. It is not clear whether that was caused by his experiences at the Front. Nevertheless, Harry failed to recover properly and was invalided out of the Army in December 1917. The next few years should have been positive ones for the family with their father back from the war. However, that was far from the case. Harry deserted his family soon after the fighting concluded, leaving his wife with three young children, Alice (8), Arthur (6) and Frank (4) and no source of income. She took in needlework to help make ends meet but that was far from sufficient for the family's needs. The family had to leave their accommodation and find somewhere they could afford. They ended up in 'the Cottage' in Croxley Hall woods. 'The Cottage' was a stable and tack room with a hay loft. About the only facility was a stone sink with one cold water tap, and a 'Kitchener' stove. It was to be their home for about ten years. Alice had to present regularly a list of every expense she made to entitle her to 5s poor relief. Life was hard. Was the Lamsley family's predicament a consequence of the war? Would Harry have deserted his family anyway without the strenuous personal impact of his time at the Front, his wounds and illness? It is hard to know.

In time, educational success offered a way out of poverty. Both Alice and Arthur gained scholarship places at grammar school. In those days, that was exceptional for children from a poor family. Just how exceptional is underlined by the entry in the Girls' School log book for 1922. The Headmistress, Miss Stanford, wrote:

> Alice Lamsley has passed the Scholarship Exam taking her to the Grammar School in September, and in honour of it all the girls brought their teas to school

111 Personal communication from Marian Lamsley-Jones, 6 July 2013

on Wednesday July 19th. We did school lessons until 3 o'clock and then went to the end of the Green. On the Boys' cricket pitch (kindly lent for the occasion) Mr Atkins, father of one of the girls, had marked out for netball so we had Blues versus Yellows in the Upper Classes, the others playing Rounders, Twenty Five, Dodge Ball etc. We had tea about five o'clock and then played again. The Old Girls arrived and then there was a spirited contest the result being 19 goals to School and 15 to Old Girls. We had a very enjoyable time, but I must confess to feeling more than limp when we reached home.

## Edgar Toms and the Leipzig War Crimes Trials 1921

Immediately after the war ended there was lingering resentment towards the Germans because of reports of their brutality, particularly towards prisoners of war. The Younger committee had interviewed 70 British soldiers, who had been captured during the Spring Offensive and managed to escape. The committee's report, published on 14 October 1918, provided evidence of the appalling conditions which prisoners suffered.[112] Although admitting that the Germans were initially overwhelmed by the numbers of prisoners taken, Younger found that prisoners were starved, deprived of adequate shelter, forced into hard manual labour under shellfire and received no medical attention when sickness was prevalent. This fed the prevailing prejudices. *The Times*' leader of 15 October was headed with a quotation from Balfour. 'Brutes they were when they began the war. Brutes they remain'.[113]

Such views were widely shared among the Allies and led to demands for German war crimes to be punished. The 1919 Treaty of Versailles stipulated that German war criminals should be tried by the Allies. However, Germany refused to extradite those accused. In 1921, it was agreed that trials should take place at the German Supreme Court in Leipzig instead, but only twelve individuals were brought to trial.

The death of Edgar Toms in the prisoner of war camp at Flavy-le-Martel provides a direct link between Croxley Green and a piece of international legal history. One of the accused was Captain Emil Mueller who was in charge of the camp for part of the time that Edgar was imprisoned there. Edgar's father, William Toms, kept the reports of the trial from the *Daily Telegraph* of 27 and 31 May 1921. The accounts must have made grim reading.

Mueller was charged with having brutally treated British prisoners of war. The *Telegraph* reported that he was also held responsible for the insanitary conditions in the camp at Flavy-le-Martel which led to an outbreak of diptheria [should this be dysentery?] that affected 1,200 of the men with fatal results in 200 cases. The *Telegraph*'s correspondent recorded that Mueller was a barrister as well as an army officer.[114] He was described as a dark, clean-shaven, heavily-built man with a cool, assured manner who spoke fluently. There were nineteen British and eighteen German witnesses and eight depositions made in London. Mueller claimed that, when he arrived, the camp was in a terrible condition because of the effects of

---

112 See *The Times,* 15 October 1918, pg 4 and pg 7
113 Arthur Balfour 1848-1930, Prime Minister 1902-05.
114 *Daily Telegraph*, Friday 27 May 1921, p.10

shellfire. He found it difficult to get the British to work and suspected a lot of malingering. Mueller admitted tying one prisoner to a stake. He suspected combined resistance by the British prisoners, discovered the ringleader and punished him as a warning to others. He denied striking prisoners.

One British witness said that, while Mueller was at the camp, prisoners had started dying and throughout May there were an average of two deaths every day. This was confirmed by another British witness who read out the diary he had kept while in the camp. Three German doctors gave evidence about conditions in the camp. One said that, when he had visited in April, he had found the camp in excellent condition. There was plenty of good water, he was favourably impressed by the kitchen arrangements and the prisoners looked well. But, when he returned in May, conditions were much worse and there was a great deal of sickness. The second doctor said that in May the conditions were extraordinarily bad. The camp was overcrowded, the latrines were too near the barracks, the roofs and walls of the huts were not weatherproof and there was much illness. The third doctor confirmed this and commented that the water was bad and the men were poorly nourished. There were deaths every day and the only source from which prisoners were provided with fresh clothing was from the uniforms stripped from their dead comrades.

Claud Mullins, a London barrister, attended all the trials as interpreter for the British mission and published an account in 1921.[115] Mullins was impressed by the fairness of the court despite strong opposition to the trials from the German public. His account gives a more complex picture than the *Telegraph* reports. The Germans had taken over the camp at Flavy-le-Martel from the British during the March offensive. The British army had used it for the temporary reception of German prisoners of war. It was in a marshy and devastated area just behind the front line and it was clearly unfit for human occupation when the British were in charge. Mueller took over the camp in this condition but the situation for the British prisoners became even worse. Over a thousand men were kept in sheds originally designed for 300 and they had to sleep on the wet ground. Sanitation was totally inadequate and all the wells nearby were ruined. The German army was desperate to make use of prisoner labour to maintain supplies to its forces. Consequently, prisoners were kept at Flavy-le-Martel rather than being transferred to healthier sites. Within a month at least 500 men were suffering from dysentery and there were many deaths. Their plight was worsened by being required to undertake strenuous work in their weakened state. *The Times* reported that the Public Prosecutor had applied for a sentence of 15 months imprisonment.[116] Nevertheless, Mueller was strongly defended by two German generals who acted as military experts at the trial.

On 31 May, the *Telegraph* reported the Court President's statement that no blame could be attached to the defendant for the conditions in the camp, nor was he guilty of dishonourable conduct or heartlessness towards the prisoners.[117] He was an energetic and conscientious officer who discharged his duty. The Court found that he had tried his best to improve the situation but was constrained by the demands of

115 Claud Mullins, *The Leipzig Trials*, Witherby, London (1921)
116 *The Times,* 30 May 1921, p. 10
117 *Daily Telegraph*, Tuesday 31 May 1921, p. 12

the German high command and by the lack of food and other supplies, owing to the Allied blockade of Germany. However, the Court found that his treatment of the prisoners was harsh and severe. There was no mutiny among the prisoners justifying severe measures, nor any trace of disobedience. The president said that the worst of all was sending sick prisoners to work. The defendant was guilty of striking prisoners on several occasions and permitting them to be ill-treated by guards in his presence. He had also deliberately ridden a horse into the ranks of the prisoners. He was sentenced to six months' imprisonment. Mueller had left Flavy-le-Martel on 5 May. Edgar Toms died a month later.

British commentators felt that the verdict was ridiculously lenient and that the trial process did nothing to compensate for the bitterness left behind by the war. At the same time, the Allied blockade of Germany and the chaotic conditions behind the German front line in 1918 meant that prisoners of war were bound to suffer. Moreover, the war crimes process took no account of atrocities carried out by the Allies. Neither side was satisfied.

# IN MEMORY

Already in 1915, the people of Croxley Green had taken their first steps to commemorate the war that was transforming their world. A list of those serving in the armed forces was prepared and the first village event of remembrance took place in November that year.

For bereaved families there was no body to bury and no grave so they needed other ways to focus their grief. Some used the 'in memoriam' columns of the local newspaper. George and Fanny Mead of 179 New Road lost two of their sons. They placed the following memorials in the paper:

> 28 April 1917. In loving memory of Lance-Corporal Ernest Mead, who died of wounds received in action on April 11th 1917, aged 23 years.
> 'Sleep on, dear boy, the strife for you is o'er.
> Nobly you did your duty and your life you gave,
> Leaving your loved ones with sad hearts and sore,
> While you are lying in a lonely grave.'

> 1 June 1918. In loving memory of our dear son Corporal Edwin Frederick Mead, KRRC, died of wounds 23rd May 1918.
> 'Out in a far off distant land, under the starlit skies,
> There amidst more silent graves is where our dear boys lie.
> Oh, that we could have clasped their hands
> and kissed them as they died,
> Or could only have heard the loving words,
> 'Dear Mum and Dad, good-bye.''
> From his sorrowing Mum, Dad, Brother and Sisters.

John and Mary Clarke lived in Scots Hill. Mary had lost three sons in the war. Their surname was Smart and, since they are not mentioned on the Croxley memorials, it is possible that they never lived in Croxley Green. She placed the following in the *Observer* of 3 November 1916 and a similar notice two years later:

> In loving remembrance of the dearly-beloved sons of Mrs Clarke, Scots Hill, killed in action – Albert, October 27th 1914, John, November 3rd 1914, Charlie, June 19th 1915.[118]
> 'Somewhere in France two bodies lie and one in the Dardanelles.'
> Three years have passed but not forgotten by their mother.

118. Private Albert Smart, 2nd Bedfordshires died on 31 October 1914 and Private John Smart, 1st Northamptonshires died on 3 November 1914. Both are remembered on the Menin Gate, Ypres. I have not been able to trace Charlie.

*The Lion and Eagle in the rose garden of Three Rivers House, Rickmansworth*

The newspaper continued to serve as a memorial for many years. For example, on 3 November 1923 there were the following entries from Croxley Green families:

GROOM – In loving remembrance of Fred, dearly loved eldest son of Mr and Mrs R Groom, Yorke Road, who died of wounds in France, Nov 3, 1916. Never forgotten by those who loved him, For there is a link death can not sever, love and remembrance are for ever. From Mum, Dad and Ron.

NEWBERRY – In ever loving memory of our dear son, Gunner S W Newberry, who fell in action Nov 3rd 1917 aged 25 years.
'In every pang that rends the heart,
The Man of Sorrows has a part,
He sympathises with our grief,
And to the sufferer sends relief.'
From his loving Mum and Dad: Mr and Mrs M Newberry, Duke of York.

SIRETT – In ever loving memory of John Belgrove Sirett, RAF, who passed away November 2nd 1918, aged 30. Always in our thoughts.

## Local War Memorials and the beginning of a tradition

With the end of the fighting there was a desire for a more permanent memorial to the dead. The King instituted national remembrance on 11 November 1919. For the first time, everyone in Croxley Green and beyond kept two minutes silence at the eleventh hour of the eleventh day of the eleventh month, 1919 (*WO* 15 November 1919).

The people of Watford began raising funds for the Peace Memorial Hospital and there was an active debate in Rickmansworth about what sort of memorial would be appropriate.[119] Croxley Green was part of the Rickmansworth Urban District Council area. William Newall of Redheath, who had lost two of his sons in the conflict, pushed hard for a memorial statue. Others had suggested some kind of public facility, such as a reading room or a contribution towards the Watford hospital. But Newall was having none of that. In a letter to the *Observer* he said that the object of a war memorial ought to be to stir the feelings of the onlookers, to keep alive the memory of those splendid young fellows who went

*All Saints' shrine erected in the church.*

out the moment war was declared to serve their God, their King and their country (*WO* 4 January 1919). He argued that only a heroic figure would arouse such sentiments. The Council's committee agreed with him and Newall introduced the council to an eminent sculptor, George Frampton RA. He in turn put forward an up and coming talent, William Reid Dick, whose design of the lion crushing an eagle was eventually accepted.[120]

Meanwhile, in Croxley Green, All Saints' church moved the shrine from the

119  See Geoff Saul, 'The Lion and Eagle', Rickmansworth Historical Society Newsletter 39, (December 1997)
120  Reid Dick also designed the Bushey war memorial.  The Rickmansworth and Bushey memorials helped to establish his reputation for monumental scullpture.  See Sarah Crellin, 'Dick, Sir William Reid (1879-1961), Oxford Dictionary of National Biography, OUP 2004 online edition accessed 13 May 2014.

churchyard into the church, where it still stands. It was unveiled there on 15 June 1919 (*WO* 21 June 1919). Shelves were provided for people to leave floral tributes. The shrine marks those known to have been killed with a Maltese cross (46); a W for those wounded (62); M for those missing (3, all of whom died); and P for those taken prisoner (7). It is not known when the final listings were prepared but it is likely to have been around the time that the shrine was moved.

In November 1919, All Saints' held the customary remembrance service for those who had died in the war on All Souls' day, 2 November. The *Observer* records that, earlier in the year, at the Peace Celebration, the headmaster of the Boys' School, H T Wilson, had proposed that an oak tree should be planted on the Green in memory of those men from the village who had died in the war. So on 2 November, a large crowd gathered on the Green opposite the end of New Road, where the tree was to be planted. Two previous vicars, Rev Donnell and Rev Wells took part in the ceremony. The tree was carried from the church preceded by the choir, clergy and band of the Dickinson Institute. They sang a hymn about the suffering soldiers of the church and Rev Wells read out the names of the 49 men from the village then known to have died. Mr Gudgin played the 'Last Post' to conclude the ceremony (*WO* 8 November 1919).

In Rickmansworth, the Council set a budget of £2,000 but it is not known how much their memorial actually cost. Nor is it known exactly how the list of names was compiled. It was probably based on proposals from committees established in the various parts of the Council area, including Croxley Green, which were then brought together under the supervision of the Council Surveyor, Albert Freeman. There are 194 names on the memorial, of which 53 also appear on the Croxley Green memorial. William Newall wanted it to be sited on Fortune Common at the bottom of Scots Hill, where he would pass it regularly. However, in June 1921 the Council decided to place the memorial on the corner of Ebury Road, west of the town. It was dedicated at the end of July and used for the Armistice Day commemoration on Friday 11 November 1921. Subsequent road improvements have displaced the plinth into the grounds of St Mary's church while the statue, thought to be too martial for the church, now stands in the rose garden at Three Rivers House.

John Dickinson and Co erected a company memorial at Apsley and then did the same at Croxley Mills. It was unveiled on 8 December 1922 by the Managing Director, R H Ling, and dedicated by Rev Blois Bisshopp. On the platform with them were worthies from the firm including A Beck, lately of the VTC and now Chief Fire Officer, and the recently retired manager, Charles Barton-Smith. But also in prominent positions at the ceremony were two of the old Croxley Church Lads, Jack Brown MM and John Gudgin, the bugler. 23 of the names commemorated are also on the Croxley Green memorial. The plaque is now on the south wall of All Saints' church and a smaller replacement of the original memorial cross sits outside the pavilion at the Croxley Guild of Sport.

Compared to the other local memorials, there is tantalisingly little written evidence about the origins of the memorial stones on the Green. Unfortunately, the magazines from All Saints' church are missing for the postwar period. In 1920, the *Observer*

*John Dickinson & Co's memorial at Croxley Mills 1922*

reported that the Armistice Day ceremony was held at the memorial oak. In November 1921, the *Observer* mentioned the sale of poppies in Croxley but had no reference to other aspects of commemoration, nor are there any reports of Croxley Green in the *Observer* during November 1922. The British Legion was established in 1921 but there are no records of the Croxley branch surviving from that period.

The Headmistress of Croxley Girls' School, Miss Stanford, made no entries in the school's log book relating to remembrance events in 1919, 1920 or 1921, but she wrote the following in November 1922. 'Friday Nov 10th we learned words and tune of 'How sleep the brave', 'God of our Fathers', 'Let us now praise famous men', and made laurel ropes in preparation for Armistice Day. This fell on Saturday but the majority of the children came to school and processed to the Memorial Oak.'

The undated photographs overleaf show the young oak tree in the middle of railings with the memorial stones in front. There are references to the memorial in both the *Observer* and the log book of Croxley Girls' School but they are capable of different interpretations. The newspaper reported that the Croxley Green branch of the British Legion promoted a competitive race for boys aged 12 to 14 on 1 July 1923 (*WO* 30 June and 28 July 1923). The trophy, the Legion Cross Country Memorial Cup, was presented 'to perpetuate the memory of those who left the village for King and country

*The memorial oak tree and railings complete with war memorial stones,
on the Green soon after it was erected.*

in the great war, 1914-1919'. The race was intended to be an annual event. The course covered three miles starting and finishing at 'the Memorial', and running down Baldwins Lane to Croxley Green Station and returning up Rickmansworth Road [i.e. what we know now as Watford Road] and New Road. Harry George Kerr of Dickinson Square came first in 18.5 minutes. 'Neggy' Wilson was involved in organising the race. Then on 10 November 1923 the *Observer* reported that All Saints' had commemorated 'the fallen' on Sunday 4 November and announced a short service would be held 'at the War Memorial' on Armistice Day itself. The phrase 'at the War Memorial' implies that the stones were then in place but that is not conclusive.

The next relevant entry in the Girls' School log book is in 1924, when the headmistress wrote, 'On Monday Nov 10th Standard 7 made laurel festoons for the railings round the Memorial Oak on the Green. On Armistice Day we had our annual service round the oak at 11 o'clock, the children singing, 'How sleep the brave', 'Let us now praise famous men' and reading the names of the fallen'. Miss Stanford made similar notes in the log book for 1925 and 1926. The girls making laurel festoons for the railings became a regular feature of the commemoration event. Miss Stanford died in 1930 and her successor wrote, 'On Monday November 10th [1930] the senior girls made eleven chains of laurel leaves each a yard long to put on the iron fence around the war memorial on the Green'. We can be confident that the memorial was complete by then but exactly when the stones joined the tree inside the railings remains open to conjecture.

There is a strong local tradition that 'Neggy' Wilson, headmaster of the Boys' School, was the driving force for the Croxley Green memorial. A note to a photograph in Croxley Green library states that he obtained the stones for the memorial from

*Croxley Green war memorial soon after it was erected*

Croxley Mills. This seems entirely plausible, although there is no contemporary written evidence. He would have known most of the men who died as his pupils.

It is not known exactly how the memorial list of 57 names was compiled. The Rickmansworth list was probably the starting point and four names are added (F N Clarke, A A Pettifer, W R Sims and J Stokes). There is a framed list of 55 names in All Saints' church, next to the shrine, which omits, probably by mistake, the names of two men whose brothers were also killed. It may be significant that the names on the top two stones of the memorial are arranged in date order of death but from B Bastin downwards there is no obvious ordering. The four names not on the Rickmansworth memorial are all in the bottom two rows. Moreover, the bottom row is not even aligned with those above, as if the designer was waiting for another name to add. This suggests that the last names were afterthoughts. Appendix 2 compares the names from the various memorials. All but two (Sims and Stokes) have been identified in the pages of this book. However, the memorial on the Green is not necessarily the last word. There are others with a claim to be included, notably Sir Guy Calthrop and Robert Duley.

Croxley men were also recorded on memorials erected by their employers, not just John Dickinson and Co Ltd. For example, Wilfred Warn was recorded on a plaque erected inside the Croxley Green Co-operative store and Edgar Toms was recorded on a tablet at the Local Government Board in Whitehall. Local societies erected war memorials as well. Three Rivers Museum has the memorial of the local branch of the

Oddfellows' Friendly Society which includes a number of Croxley names.

In addition, there are a few individual memorials locally.  The Newalls erected an impressive monument in All Saints' church to their two sons. There are six graves of Croxley men in Chorleywood Road cemetery, Rickmansworth.

# AND THE LEAVES OF THE TREE WERE FOR THE HEALING OF THE NATIONS

41 ex-members of the Croxley Green Church Lads' Brigade had enlisted at the beginning of the war (see Appendix 1). By the end, 11 of them were dead and at least 3 suffered so badly from wounds that they were medically discharged. Overall, more than 400 Croxley men joined the armed services and at least 57 died. Many more were wounded physically and mentally. Every family had been affected by the war in one way or another.

The quotation chosen for the memorial inscription comes from the book of Revelation, chapter 22, verse 2. It is part of St John's vision of a new heaven and new earth at the end of time, when God will wipe away every tear and there will be an end to death. For the people of Croxley Green in 1919, the memorial oak tree was a symbol. It represented life, patriotism and hope for the future.

| APPENDIX 1. EX-MEMBERS OF CROXLEY GREEN CHURCH LADS' BRIGADE WHO ENLISTED IN 1914 | | | |
|---|---|---|---|
| Surname | Christian Name(s) | Unit at enlistment | 1918 |
| ADAMS | FREDERICK | 16 KRRC | Rifleman 16 KRRC |
| ARNOLD | FRANK HENRY | 16 KRRC | **Killed 2/7/16** |
| ASPREY | DAVID | Royal Engineers | Corporal Royal Engineers |
| ASPREY | EDWARD | Royal Engineers | Second Lieutenant, RE |
| ATKINS | OLIVER | 16 KRRC | Driver, Motor Transport, Army Service Corps |
| BARTON-SMITH | ARTHUR | 16 KRRC | Rifleman 17 KRRC |
| BEAMENT (MM) | JACK | 16 KRRC | Rifleman 16 KRRC |
| BROWN (MM) | JACK | 16 KRRC | |
| CHAPMAN | HARRY | 16 KRRC | **Killed 21/9/17** |
| DEARMAN | ALFRED | Royal Horse Artillery | |
| ELBOURNE | FREDERICK | Norfolks | **Killed 13/10/15** |
| ELEMENT | HERBERT | 16 KRRC | Medically discharged (unfit) 17/12/14 |
| GOODMAN (MM) | WILLIAM | Norfolks | **Killed 16/10/16** |
| GOODMAN | JOHN VICTOR | 16 KRRC | **Killed 2/1/16** |
| GRAVESTOCK | CECIL | 16 KRRC | **Killed 15/7/16** |
| GRAY | FREDERICK | Herts Light Infantry | Sergeant, Chinese Labour Coy. |
| GUNNELL | BENJAMIN | 16 KRRC | Lance-Corporal, 113th Labour Coy. |
| GUNNELL | ALBERT | 16 KRRC | Medically discharged (wounds) 28/2/17 |
| HOBBS | ARTHUR | 16 KRRC | Lance-Corporal 8th Royal Irish |
| HOBBS | FRANK | Bedfordshires | **Killed** 16/11/16 |
| HOWARD | ARTHUR | 16 KRRC | Medically discharged (wounds) 3/5/19 |
| HOWARD | FRANK | 16 KRRC | Rifleman 16 KRRC |

| Surname | Christian Name(s) | Unit at enlistment | 1918 |
|---|---|---|---|
| JONES | FRANK | 16 KRRC | |
| KING | HERBERT | 16 KRRC | Private, Royal Engineers |
| KING | SIDNEY | 16 KRRC | Medically discharged? |
| LYONS | JAMES | 16 KRRC | **Killed 14/11/16** |
| LYONS | TOM | 16 KRRC | Corporal, 382nd Labour company |
| MOORE | SIDNEY | 16 KRRC | |
| NOBBS | WILLIAM | | |
| PEEK | ARTHUR | 16 KRRC | Private 147th Labour Company |
| PUTMAN | ARTHUR | 16 KRRC | |
| QUELCH | FREDERICK | 16 KRRC | Medically discharged (unfit) 17/12/14 |
| RAGGETT (MM) | ARTHUR | 16 KRRC | Acting Corporal 6 KRRC |
| ROGERS | CHARLES | 16 KRRC | **Killed 15/7/16** |
| SILLS | FRANK | 16 KRRC | Medically discharged (wounds) 24/8/17 |
| STRUGNELL | CHARLES ALFRED | | **Killed 1/7/16** |
| THORPE | GEORGE | 16 KRRC | |
| TOMS | ROBERT | 16 KRRC | Private, 2nd Northumberland Fusiliers |
| WARN | WILFRED | 16 KRRC | **Killed 22/7/16** |
| WARN | ALFRED | 16 KRRC | Medically discharged (unfit) |
| WEBB | WILLIAM | 16 KRRC | |
| | | | 11 killed, 6 or 7 medically discharged |

APPENDIX 1. EX-MEMBERS OF CROXLEY GREEN CHURCH LADS' BRIGADE WHO ENLISTED IN 1914

| SURNAME | FORENAME / INITIAL | All Saints shrine | Dickinson Memorial |
|---|---|---|---|
| Croxley Green memorial | | June 1919 | December 1922 |
| ALLAWAY | Albert | A Alloway (not recorded as killed) | A Allaway |
| ARNOLD | Frank Henry | F Arnold | F H Arnold |
| BASTIN | Benjamin | B.Bastin (missing) | |
| BEAMENT | Stanley William | S W Beament (missing) | S Beament |
| BRICKELL | James Gatehouse | J C Brickell | |
| CARTER | William | W Carter (not recorded as killed but E Carter is recorded as killed) | W Carter |
| CHAPMAN | Harry | H Chapman | H Chapman |
| CLARK | Frederick Nathaniel | F N Clark | |
| DEAN | Lewis John | L J Dean (missing) | |
| DORROFIELD | William George | W G Dorrofield (wounded) | W G Dorrofield |
| ELBOURNE | Frederick George | F G Elbourne | F G Elbourne |
| ELEMENT | Walter E | W E Element | W Element |
| ELEMENT | Sidney Albert | S A Element | |
| GARDNER | John Henry | J Gardner | |
| GODDARD | Albert | A Goddard | |
| GOODMAN | John Victor | J V Goodman | |
| GOODMAN | William | W Goodman | W Goodman |
| GRAVESTOCK | Cecil | C W Gravestock | C G Gravestock |
| GROOM | Frederick Robert | F R Groom | |
| HOBBS | Frank | F Hobbs | F Hobbs |
| JEFFERY | Herbert James | NOT LISTED | |
| JEFFORD | Arthur William | A W Jefford | |
| KEMPSTER | Albert | NOT LISTED | |
| LYONS | James Albert | A J Lyons | |
| MASON | Herbert Bertram | H B Mason | |
| MEAD | Ernest | E Mead | E Mead |
| MEAD | Edwin Frederick | E F Mead | E F Mead |
| NEALE | Maurice | M Neale | M Neale |
| NEWALL | Leslie | L Newall | |
| NEWALL | Nigel | N Newall | |
| NEWBERRY | Samuel William | S W Newberry | |
| NEWBERRY | John Henry | J M Newberry | |

| | | All Saints shrine | Dickinson Memorial |
|---|---|---|---|
| **SURNAME** | **FORENAME / INITIAL** | | |
| *Croxley Green memorial* | | *June 1919* | *December 1922* |
| **NEWMAN** | John | J Newman | |
| **OWEN** | Arthur John | A J Owen | |
| **PARGETER** | Arthur Baylis | A A Pargeter | |
| **PEEK** | Lionel Aslin | L Peek | L A Peek |
| **PETTIFER** | Alfred Albert | NOT LISTED (R Pettifer listed) | A A Pettifer |
| **PITKIN** | Leonard | L Pitkin | L Pitkin |
| **RANDALL** | Frederick | H F Randall | |
| **REVELL** | John Josiah | John Revell | J J Revell |
| **REVELL** | James | Jas Revell | |
| **ROGERS** | Charles | C Rogers | C Rogers |
| **SANSOM** | Frederick John | F Sansom | |
| **SIMS\*** | Walter R | W R Sims (not recorded as killed) | |
| **SIRETT** | John Belgrove | J B Sirett | |
| **SOUTHAM** | David | D Southam | D Southam |
| **STOKES\*** | John | J Stokes (not recorded as killed) | |
| **STRUGNELL** | Alfred Charles | A C Strugnell | |
| **THOMAS** | Francis Albert | F Thomas | F Thomas |
| **TOMS** | Arthur | A Toms | |
| **TOMS** | Edgar John | E J Toms | |
| **WALKER** | Fredrick John | J Walker | |
| **WARN** | Wilfred | W Warn | |
| **WEBB** | Charles | C Webb (not recorded as Killed) | C Webb |
| **WHEELER** | Cecil George | C G Wheeler | |
| **WOOLLAMS** | William Arthur | W Wollams | W Woollams |
| **WOOLLAMS** | Joseph | J Woollams | |
| **57** | | 46 Killed plus 3 missing = 49 | 23 |
| **Notes** | Names are shown in the two left hand columns as they appear in this book. The war memorials on the Green and in Rickmansworth only have initials. The written list in All Saints' church has first names and surnames. There are a number of discrepancies. The war memorials on the Green and Rickmansworth have Alloway, not Allaway. All Saints' written list has Alfred, not Albert, Kempster. The memorial on the Green lists 4 names not on the Rickmansworth memorial (Clark, Pettifer, Sims and Stokes) and 2 names not on the All Saints' written list (William Goodman and John Revell). Three of the names on the Croxley Green memorial are not listed on All Saints' shrine (Jeffery, Kempster and A Pettifer). 6 are not recorded on the shrine as killed or missing (Alloway, W Carter, Dorrofield, Sims, Stokes and Webb) but E Carter is recorded as killed. | | |
| **2\* not identified** | Walter Richard Sims is listed on the absent voters' list as living in Yorke Road, Private 265112, 3rd County of London Yeomanry. Death records have not been identified for Sims or for J Stokes. | | |
| **3 May 2014** | From research by Jim Hughes, Richard Lee and Brian Thomson, with thanks to Neil Wheeler | | |

**APPENDIX 2 (continued). CROXLEY GREEN MEN KILLED IN THE FIRST WORLD WAR AS RECORDED ON LOCAL MEMORIALS (see end notes)**

# Bibliography

## First World War

Simon Forty (ed.), *World War One, A Visual Encyclopedia*, PRC Publishing, 2002
Martin Gilbert, *First World War*, Weidenfield and Nicholson, 1994
Lyn Macdonald, *Somme,* Michael Joseph, Great Britain, 1983.
Terry Norman, *The Hell They Called High Wood,* Patrick Stevens, 1984.
Gordon L Routledge, *Gretna's Secret War*, Bookcase 1999
Ivor Slocombe, 'Recruitment into the Armed Forces during the first World War. the work of the Military Tribunals in Wiltshire, 1915-1918', *The Local Historian*, May 2000.
Hew Strachan (ed.), *Oxford Illustrated History of the First World War,* Oxford University Press, 1998
Richard Van Emden and Steve Humphries, *All Quiet on the Home Front*, Headline Book Publishing London, 2003.
Ray Westlake, *Tracing British Battalions on the Somme*, Leo Cooper, Great Britain, 1994.

## Croxley Green

All Saints' Parish Magazine
Beryl Carrington, *Care in Crisis: Hertfordshire British Red Cross 1907-1994*, Baron Birch, 1995.
Croxley Green National School Log Book.
John Dickinson and Co. Ltd., *War Time in a Paper Mill 1914-18.*
Joan Evans, *The Endless Web. J. Dickinson and Co. 1804 to 1954.* Jonathan Cape, London, 1955.
Patrick Moore, *A History of Redheath and York House School*, Triflower Press 2010
J B Nunn, *The Book of Watford*, Pageprint (Watford), 1987.
Frank Paddick, *A Village Boyhood*, Rickmansworth Historical Society, 2012
Oliver Phillips, *Watford in the 20th Century, Volume 1*, Watford Observer, June 2011
*Rickmansworth Historical Society Newsletter*
Neil Wheeler, *The First World War Memorials and Soldiers of Croxley Green*, Report for Open University, 1995.

## Church Lads' Brigade

Robin Bolton, *Looking back, the story of the Church Lads' and Church Girls' Brigade*, 2002

## General Reference

Census 1911, Kelly's and Peacock's Directories, Register of electors 1918
*Watford Illustrated,*
*West Herts and Watford Observer*

# Subject Index

# Index of Names

157